SIMPLY SOUTHERN

WITH A DASH OF KOSHER SOUL

Memphis' Jewish community has been on the American Jewish map for over one hundred years and the Margolin Hebrew Academy has been educating students since 1949. Fourth generation Memphians now return to our community, seeking the warm, vibrant Memphis of their childhood and finding little has changed. Our editors recognize these young cooks and hope this book inspires them to cook "Simply Southern With A Dash Of Kosher Soul." We look forward to tasting your food and eagerly anticipate your spin on the recipes you create to meet your needs as 21st century women. However, we dedicate *Simply Southern with a Dash of Kosher Soul* to the numerous women whose culinary accomplishments have defined kosher Southern cuisine. Their commitment to the school, no less than their commitment in the kitchen, has enabled us to collaboratively write this cookbook.

ISBN: 978-0-615-32320-6

Copyright © 2009

Reorder — 1-866-715-7667

simplysoutherncookbook.net

First Printing, December 2009, 5,000 copies

WIMMER
COOKBOOKS

A CONSOLIDATED GRAPHICS COMPANY

800.548.2537   wimmerco.com

2

TABLE OF CONTENTS

Recipes

This section is in memory of our parents
Beatrice and Ben Leach z"l ■ Ann and Jacob Wruble z"l
Your gracious spirits and generous hearts have left an indelible mark on us and our community.
Dedicated with Love, by Diane and Larry Wruble

HISTORY OF OUR SCHOOL....

Located in the heart of the vibrant Jewish community of Memphis, Tennesse, the Margolin Hebrew Academy / Feinstone Yeshiva of the South is a warm, community-centered Orthodox Day School committed to instilling within its students a love of Judaism, the State of Israel, and the Jewish people while simultaneously providing the best in secular and college preparatory studies. Since its inception in 1949, MHA / FYOS has fostered passion and commitment for Jewish learning and for a Jewish lifestyle, while imbuing its students with a deep rooted sense of communal responsibility and the tools for a lifetime of success.

The 210 students of the MHA / FYOS are divided into four divisions, all located on the seven acre school campus in East Memphis. The Leach Early Childhood Program begins with 3 year olds and blends developmentally appropriate skill and content learning with a rich introduction to Jewish life and the Hebrew language in an integrated, center-based, hands-on learning environment infused with love, nurturing, and fun.

The co-educational Lower School division features a caring yet rigorous environment designed to meet the diverse needs of the Memphis Jewish community and highly attuned to the individual needs of every student. Its innovative curricula and extracurricular programming actively nurture curiosity and creativity, community and camaraderie, while facilitating maximal student learning in a full array of General and Judaic studies.

The two High School divisions of MHA / FYOS, the Cooper Yeshiva High School for Boys and the Goldie Margolin High School for Girls, provide a warm, supportive yet challenging single gender environment for young men and women to grow academically, emotionally, and religiously. Their residential programs offer an Orthodox boarding school option for students from across the globe so as to increase the diversity of its student body and to facilitate the formation of new student friendships. Through an unwavering dedication to educational excellence in all subject areas, leadership opportunities, as well as community building initiatives, the high schools prepare their students for successful matriculation to the finest universities, yeshivot, and seminaries in the world.

SIMPLY SOUTHERN

With a Dash of Kosher Soul

SPONSORS

DIAMOND LEVEL
Mildred Krasner
Dena and Gary Wruble

PLATINUM LEVEL
Frances and Herschel Rosenberg

CORPORATE LEVEL

GOLD LEVEL
Julie and Marty Belz
The Cooper Family
Carol and Harry Friedman
Paul Friedman
Lisa and Seth Kaufman
Joyce and David Krasner
Laurie and Sheldon Smith
Essie and Mike Stein
Cindi and Joe Weinstein
Rochelle and Ed Wiener
Diane and Larry Wruble

SILVER LEVEL
Amy and Daniel Gibber
Chumie and Kevin Rosenberg
Pearl Katz z"l by
Chavi and Ronnie Katz
Avigail and R. Benjamin Wolmark
by
Rivkie and R. Mordechai Wolmark

BRONZE LEVEL
Anonymous
Anonymous
Debra and Cary Califf
Janis and Brian Kiel
Ahava and Edward Lang
Dale Shields and Malcolm Lindy
Karen and Stephen Moss
Julie and Marc Sorin
Elaine and Irvin Skopp
Ellen and Ellis Tavin

CHEFS LEVEL

Amy and Solomon Ades
Barbara and Nathan Ades
Odette Ades
Sondra and Marvin Ballin
Sarah and Alex Baum
Joan and Phillip Baum
Shelby and Lee Baum
Tania and Jonathan Blotner
Bert Bornblum
Kendel and Marc Bornstein
Pat and Sam Chafetz
Sue Cohn
Barbara Epstein
Malki and Rabbi Aaron Feigenbaum
Tamara Folz M.D.

Natalie and Jerry Frager
Evelyn and Marlin Graber
Tova and Roy Graber
Eileen and Norman Itkowitz
Joanne and Joel Kahane
Diane and Michael Kaplan
Kosher Cajun
Rochelle and Jerry Kutliroff
Phylis and Sandy Levine
Julie Lindy
Sue Ann and Bernard Lipsey
Shani and Rabbi Uriel Lubetski
Gary Mantell
Brenda and Morris Massry
Elise and Greg Meyer
Louise Morris

Mindy Morris
Jeri and Mitch Moskovitz
Robin and Sergio Musicante
Cindy Osbourne
Melissa and Rabbi Gil Perl
Marilyn and Sydney Pollack
Tracy and Asher Rapp
Nili Sauer
Dessie Sewell
Erika and Andrew Sigel
Leah Jean and Richard Snyder
Emily and Alvin Steinberg
Gwen and Stephen Wachtel
Craig Wiener
Trica and Andy Woodman

CONTRIBUTORS

We gratefully acknowledge and celebrate the contributions of the many people who have given their time, recipes, stories and guidance in putting together **Simply Southern with a Dash of Kosher Soul**. *It has been a labor of love. We also hope we have not overlooked any contributors inadvertently.*

Tania Addess	Debbie Gibber	Sandra Osdoba
Odette Ades	Bobby Glover	Shelly Ostrow
Lisa Bacaner	Suri Goldman	Melissa Perl
Greta Baum	Evelyn Graber	Carley Peven
Joan Baum	Pammy Graber	Marilyn Pollack
Shelby Baum	Tova Graber	Barbara Radinsky
Suzanne Baum	Cori Grant	Tami Radinsky
Julie Belz	Miriam Greenblatt	Tracy Rapp
Leslie Berkelhammer	Janice Habbaz	Eva Rosenberg
Nina Blockman	Jan Hanover	Frances Rosenberg
Tania Blotner	Diane Harkavy	Chumie Rosenberg
Julie Boshwit	Charlette Hearne	Lauren Roth
Aliza Braverman	Eileen Itkowitz	Karen Rubenstein
Jason Braverman	Robin Joyce	Patricia Safier
Rivka Braverman	Joanne Kahane	Sherri Samuels
Rachel Brown	Anna Kaminetzky	Adina Samberg
Wanda Burch	Anat Kampf	Linda Schlesinger
Jill Buring	Abbe Kaplan	Aliyah Schneider
Debra Califf	Diane Kaplan	Davida Schultz
Karen Carrier	Esther Katz	Dessie Sewel
Pat Chafetz	Estaline Katz	Beth Sherman
Eileen Cherny	Lisa Kaufman	Erika Sigel
John Clark	Janis Kiel	Laurie Smith
Hazel Cohen	Rivki Klein	Leah Jean Snyder
Aileen Cooper	Mildred Krasner	Angela Snyder
Laurie Cooper	Aviva Krupp	Nancy Somer
Tova Cooper	Ricki Krupp	Emily Steinberg
Bernice Cooper	Rochelle Kutliroff	Arlene Strauss
Frieda Cooper	Harriet Levin	Sue Strong
Madelyne Daneman	Joyce Levine	Ellen Tavin
Mimi David	Phylis Levine	Gwen Wachtel
Jill Dempsey	Evan Levy	Debby Weinstein
Ray Edelman	Aviva Lewis	Penina Wender
Cindy Ehrenkranz	Julie Lindy	Razelle Wender
Tami Eiseman	Sue Ann Lipsey	Sally Wender
Sarah Emerson	Dinah Makowsky	Ellie Williams
Rina Emerson	Millie Malkin	Shulamis Weinfeld
Jan Epstein	Alyne Matz	Rochelle Wiener
Vikki Evans	Frances McCoy	Avigail Wolmark
Galila Finegold	Karen Monsein	Tricia Woodman
Bilha Finkelstein	Louise Morris	Nancy Wright
Natalie Frager	Mindy Morris	Alyssa Wruble
Noreen Freiden	Valerie Morris	Dena Wruble
Sherry Gans	Jeri Moskovitz	Diane Wruble
Sandy Gersten	Karen Moss	Simone Wruble
Amy Gibber	Beverly Noffel	Gila Zelig

ACKNOWLEDGEMENTS

EDITORS-IN-CHIEF
Tracy Rapp
Dena Wruble

ASSISTANT CO-EDITORS
Tania Blotner
Tova Cooper

RECIPE EDITORS
Tova Cooper
Tova Graber
Shayna Somer
Gila Zelig

WRITERS
Talia Kaufman
Julie Lindy
Gil Perl
Vicki Tyler
Talya Tsuna

STORYTELLERS
Joan Baum
Julie Belz
Tania Blotner
Bernice Cooper
Noreen Freiden
Evelyn Graber
Miriam Greenblatt

Gilbert Halpern
Ricki Krupp
Joyce Levine
Sue Ann Lipsey
Eva and Meyer Rosenberg
Karen Rubenstein
Bettie Thomas
Rochelle Wiener
Diane Wruble

FUNDRAISING
Julie Belz
Tania Blotner
Noreen Freiden
Lisa Kaufman
Tracy Rapp
Frances and Herschel
    Rosenberg
Rochelle and Ed Wiener
Dena and Gary Wruble
Diane Wruble

FUNDRAISING SECRETARY
Cindi Weinstein

TREASURER
Frances Rosenberg
Dena Wruble

**MARKETING AND
PUBLIC RELATIONS**
Jonathan Blotner
Eileen Itkowitz
Lisa Kaufman
Phylis Levine
Gil Perl
Asher Rapp
Linda Schlesinger

DESIGN AND LAYOUT
Dena Wruble
Debra Califf

SALES
Shelby Baum
Tania Blotner
Aileen Cooper
Aviva Freiden
Tracy Rapp

WEBSITE
Mindy Morris
Gershon Yarmush
Adam Wiener

In honor of the best wife, mother, and chef
Dena Wruble
You did a great job! We love you,
Gary ▪ Justin ▪ Aylssa ▪ Aaron ▪ Sophie ▪ Emma

Simply Southern cookbook acknowledges our families for their support and encouragement for this never ending project. Their sacrifices have been many with the hope that the rewards will be great. Their patience for the late night runs to the grocery, the tasting of recipes, the endless meetings and constant talk of the "cookbook" will be forever treasured.

The home cooked meal.

Few images are as inviting, wholesome and embracing. Few thoughts stimulate the palate and soothe the soul as that of a home cooked meal. And few cultures have formed so venerated a place for a home cooked meal in their respective traditions as those of the American South and the descendants of European Jewry. For the former, it was a Sunday dinner with the family or a formal evening party. It was Thanksgiving or Christmas, New Year's or Easter. For the latter it was a Friday night dinner after dark as the Sabbath set in or a Saturday lunch filled with guests. It was Passover or Sukkot, Hannukah or Purim.

In the small Jewish communities that have dotted the South for centuries — from Georgia to Louisiana, the Carolinas to Tennessee — these two legendary traditions of hospitality and home cooking have come together as one. And this book begins to tell its story…this book begins to tell our story.

Anyone who has ever had the pleasure of visiting Memphis knows of our Southern hospitality. Many are surprised to find we lack kosher restaurants. Yet, once they are guests in any of the homes in our community, they understand why we do not feel we are deprived. Entertaining is more than just an obligation for us; it is an art form and a way to bring us all together. All new neighbors are greeted with a freshly baked treat and every simcha or special occasion — from bris to bar mitzvah to wedding — is catered by community hosts. Resisting the allure of fast food and mass catering, we opt to prepare our own meals, spending hours around our dining room tables, where everyone is welcome to partake in the celebration. We take to heart the Jewish tradition of *hachnasas orchim,* welcoming guests into our homes, and give it a healthy helping of Southern charm.

We wanted to find a way to share our passion for food and entertaining, while supporting an organization that above all others has held us together. Our school, the Margolin Hebrew Academy, is truly the heart of our community. It has educated three generations of Memphians and, by nurturing our children's souls, has enabled our Jewish traditions to thrive in the Bible Belt.

The call for Southern recipes elicited over fifteen hundred responses. Ladies Auxiliary lifetime members and first year parents, newlyweds and those wed for over sixty years, bubbies and meemaws, immas and mommas answered the call, eager to share recipes, stories and secrets. There are Southern recipes turned kosher and kosher recipes turned Southern. To fully appreciate this book, you must understand: this is not an ordinary cookbook. Those looking for a list of recipes reflecting the latest trends from a certain city can look elsewhere. We do things a little differently down in Memphis. These recipes are the products of a community whose greatest joy is to entertain and whose greatest fear is that someone might go unfed. The dishes in this book are heirlooms, passed down by oral tradition, printed in our school's weekly newsletter and emailed between best friends.

These recipes provide personal glimpses into our vibrant community — a growing amalgam of Memphis families several generations strong, transplants from smaller Southern towns, and more recent emigrants from the North. They come from our community's heart, and we trust they will find a place in yours. It has taken us years to collect, test and retest, tweak and perfect these recipes. We are ready to share them with y'all; welcome into our simply Southern homes!

Appetizers & Starters

Dedicated to my wife, *Carol,* whose cooking fills me with warmth and comfort, and to our mothers, may they rest in peace, *Miriam Weber Friedman* and *Belle Ackerman Lipman,* whose delicious wholesome cooking inspired us to find the joy in home cooked meals.
Harry Friedman

In Noreen

In Noreen Freiden's family, a passion for cooking seemed to skip a generation. While Noreen's grandmother ruled the kitchen, her mother could not boil water. However, this did not stop Noreen from learning how to cook. "My grandmother was known for her gefilte fish, which took four days to prepare," she recalls. "The fish stayed in the bathtub overnight before my grandmother began to prepare it." To her grandmother, cooking was an art, and Noreen was a willing "art" student. Her grandmother taught her to prepare food without measuring and to always make a little extra- just in case. She remembers mixing her first challah dough, her grandmother encouraging her to add flour until it "felt right". Noreen uses this technique today in the cookies she makes for her grandchildren's snack on their way home from the Margolin Hebrew Academy. She has had a child, grandchild or great grandchild enrolled in the school since its inception, and she has offered tasty treats to them and their friends for many years now. These days, she is teaching her grandchildren to cook, and her philosophy remains the same: "If you put in good ingredients, you make something good."

EASY CHEESE STRAWS

Cheese Straws have been the old Southern standby cocktail snack as far back as anyone can remember. These should not be confused with breadsticks. There was not a lot of cheese available in the South in the 1800's and baking them on pastry was a way to preserve them. Since then, Southerners love to serve cheese straws to their guests not just for cocktails, but to accompany a meal.

2 sheets puff pastry, thawed
1 large egg
1 tablespoon water
¼ cup grated Parmesan cheese

¼ cup shredded Cheddar cheese
Spicy seasoning, pepper Jack cheese, pesto sauce, cayenne pepper, sesame seeds, or dried Italian dressing (optional)

Preheat oven to 400 degrees. Roll out pastry on a lightly floured surface to an 18 x 12-inch rectangle. Beat together egg and water. Brush one pastry sheet with egg wash. Combine Parmesan cheese and Cheddar cheese. Sprinkle evenly over pastry. Sprinkle with flavoring of choice. Firmly press second pastry sheet on top. Roll with rolling pin to press together. Trim edges until even. Cut pastry sheet into ⅓ to ½-inch wide strips. Twist each strip three times to form a spiral. Place on lightly greased baking sheet. Bake at 400 degrees for 20 minutes or until golden browned. Transfer to a serving platter. Serve hot or room temperature.

YIELD: 6 SERVINGS

CHEESE CRISPS

1 stick butter, softened
1 cup shredded sharp Cheddar cheese
1 cup all-purpose flour

Dash of Tabasco or Worcestershire sauce
¼-½ teaspoon cayenne pepper
1 cup crispy rice cereal

Cream butter and Cheddar cheese. Stir in flour, Tabasco, cayenne, and rice cereal. Roll mixture into 1 to 2-inch balls. Flatten each ball on baking sheet. Bake at 350 degrees for 15-20 minutes.

YIELD: 8 SERVINGS

PECAN CHEDDAR COOKIES

1 stick butter, softened	½ teaspoon cayenne pepper
2½ cups grated Cheddar cheese	⅔ cup all-purpose flour
1 egg yolk	⅔ cup chopped pecans
½ teaspoon salt	

Preheat oven to 350 degrees. Beat butter and Cheddar cheese until smooth. Beat in egg yolk, salt, cayenne, flour, and pecans into smooth dough. Roll rounded teaspoonfuls dough into balls. Arrange about 3-inches apart on greased baking sheet. Flatten each ball into a 1½-inch disk. Bake at 350 degrees for 15-18 minutes or until golden browned.

YIELD: 8 TO 10 SERVINGS

Store in airtight container for 2-3 days or freeze.

CHEDDAR OLIVES

A savory pop-in-your-mouth treat!

1 cup shredded Cheddar cheese	3 tablespoons butter, softened
½ cup all-purpose flour	20 pimento stuffed green olives,
⅛ teaspoon cayenne pepper	drained and patted dry

Preheat oven to 400 degrees. Combine Cheddar cheese, flour, and cayenne. Stir in butter until dough forms. Roll 1 tablespoon dough into ball. Press thumb into dough ball. Place olive in thumbprint. Wrap dough around olive to seal. Place balls on parchment paper-lined baking sheet. Bake at 400 degrees for 15 minutes. Serve warm.

YIELD: 6 SERVINGS

May prepare in advance, freeze and reheat.

EGGPLANT WITH A TWIST

1   **pound eggplant, sliced into ¼-inch rounds**
5   **tablespoons olive oil, divided**
2   **tablespoons vinegar**

¼   **cup chopped mint**
2   **tablespoons capers, rinsed**
¼   **teaspoon salt**
½   **teaspoon pepper**

Preheat broiler. Arrange eggplant in a single layer on a baking sheet. Brush both sides with 2 tablespoons oil. Broil about 4 inches from heat source for 6 minutes. Turn and broil an additional 6 minutes or until golden browned.

Blend 3 tablespoons oil, vinegar, mint, capers, salt, and pepper in a bowl. Chop cooled eggplant. Add to dressing and toss to coat. Marinate for at least 20 minutes.

YIELD: 6 TO 8 SERVINGS

EGGS AND CARAMELIZED ONION SALAD

12   **hard-boiled eggs**
2   **tablespoons vegetable oil**
2   **large sweet onions, chopped**

3   **tablespoons mayonnaise**
¾   **teaspoon salt**
¾   **teaspoon pepper**

Coarsely grate eggs into a bowl. Heat oil in skillet. Sauté onion until browned. Add to eggs. Stir in mayonnaise, salt, and pepper until well mixed.

YIELD: 6 TO 8 SERVINGS

FARM FRESH ROASTED TOMATOES WITH FRESH HERBS

*This dish is very versatile and is best during
the summer months when tomatoes and herbs are in season.*

2	pints cherry tomatoes, halved	1	red onion, chopped
½	cup chopped fresh basil	½	cup olive oil
¼	cup chopped fresh oregano		Pita chips

Preheat oven to 450 degrees. Combine tomatoes, basil, oregano, red onion, and oil. Mix well. Roast at 450 degrees for 1-2 hours, stirring frequently. Serve warm or chilled with pita chips.

YIELD: 8 TO 10 SERVINGS

Store in refrigerator for 1-2 weeks. Serve over pasta for a meal or pair with hummus, minted eggplant or guacamole for a first course or appetizer.

PITA CRISPS

Pita bread　　　　　　　　　　**Garlic salt**

Butter, melted

Cut pita bread in quarters. Carefully separate two layers from each quarter to give eight pieces. Brush melted butter over pita pieces. Sprinkle with garlic salt. Bake at 400 degrees 15-18 minutes or until desired crispiness.

THREE PEPPER QUESADILLAS

May also make this a meal for your family!

1 cup thinly sliced bell pepper
1 cup thinly sliced yellow pepper
1 cup thinly sliced sweet red pepper
1 cup thinly sliced onion
4 tablespoons butter
¼ teaspoon ground cumin
1 (4 ounce) can chopped green chilies, undrained
1 (8 ounce) package cream cheese, softened

1 (8 ounce) package shredded Cheddar cheese
1 (14 ounce) package flour tortillas
  Butter
  Ground cumin or chili powder to taste
1 (8 ounce) container sour cream
¼ cup salsa

Sauté all peppers and onion in butter in large skillet. Stir in cumin. Remove any liquid from skillet. Set aside. Combine chilies, cream cheese and Cheddar cheese in a separate bowl. May prepare one day in advance to this point.

To assemble quesadillas, spread 3-4 tablespoons cheese mixture on half of flour tortilla. Top with pepper/onion mixture. Fold tortilla over. Lightly spread butter over folded tortilla. Sprinkle with cumin or chili powder. Place on baking sheet. Bake at 400 degrees for 10-15 minutes or until bubbly and lightly browned. Cut into thirds or fourths. Blend sour cream and salsa. Serve as a dip with quesadillas.

YIELD: 15 SERVINGS

These quesadillas are fairly mild. If you want to boost up the heat, add jalapeños to the cheese mixture or be sure your salsa is spicy hot.

SESAME CHICKEN TOASTS

This Thai specialty is a scrumptious and original crowd pleaser!

4	boneless skinless chicken thighs	¼	cup chicken broth
1	boneless skinless chicken breast half	½	teaspoon pepper
1	egg, beaten	¼	teaspoon salt
3	green onions, finely chopped	12-15	slices white sandwich bread, crust removed and cut into 8 triangles
2	garlic cloves, minced	½	cup sesame seeds
2	tablespoons chopped cilantro		Vegetable oil

Process chicken in food processor until finely chopped. Add egg, green onion, garlic, cilantro, broth, pepper, and salt. Pulse a few times to mix well. Scatter sesame seeds onto a plate. Spread a thick layer of chicken mixture over bread pieces. Press spread side into seeds making an even covering.

Heat ½-inch oil in a skillet until hot. Quickly fry triangles for 2-3 minutes on both sides, turning once until golden browned. Drain toasts on paper towels.

YIELD: 12 SERVINGS

Toast may be prepared in advance. Store in refrigerator for 3 days or frozen up to a month. Thaw overnight in refrigerator. Reheat in hot oven for 5 minutes.

SPICY LIME FRIED CHICKEN DRUMMIES

Honey and lime juice combine to create an irresistible sauce!

5	pounds chicken drummies	1	tablespoon kosher salt
1¾	cups lime juice, divided		Vegetable oil
1	cup soymilk	2	cups all-purpose flour
2	tablespoons minced garlic	2	tablespoons Creole seasoning
1	tablespoon plus 1 teaspoon crushed red pepper, divided	1	cup honey
		2	tablespoons lime zest

Place chicken in a 1 gallon zip-top plastic bag. Combine 1½ cups lime juice, soymilk, garlic, 1 tablespoon red pepper, and salt in a bowl. Mix well. Pour marinade over chicken. Seal bag. Refrigerate at least 12 hours or overnight, turning bag occasionally.

Preheat oven to 200 degrees. Heat 2-3 inches oil in a large skillet to about 350 degrees. Drain chicken from marinade. Combine flour and seasoning in a new 1 gallon zip-top plastic bag. Place chicken in flour mixture and shake to coat. Lay chicken on a wire rack set over a baking sheet. Let rest for 20 minutes.

Fry chicken in batches about 7-9 minutes or until golden browned and beginning to float. Drain on paper-lined baking sheet. Place in oven to keep warm.

Blend ¼ cup lime juice, 1 teaspoon red pepper, honey, and lime zest in a bowl. Serve dipping sauce with drummies.

YIELD: 8 TO 10 SERVINGS

We prefer chicken drummies over wings but either one will disappear quickly. May also grill drummies!

BAR B Q PARTY FRANKS

This is a big hit at a large party, particularly if there are a lot of kids!

2	pounds frankfurters	½	cup Bar B Q sauce
1	can beer	1	cup brown sugar

Cut franks in 1 inch lengths. Mix beer, BBQ sauce and brown sugar and pour over franks. Marinate overnight. Cook over medium heat in a saucepan for 30 minutes. Use a large saucepan, as they will expand as they cook. Serve in a bowl with a small amount of sauce. Keep warm and serve with toothpicks.

CHICKEN CAKES
WITH RÉMOULADE SAUCE

This is a great idea for leftover chicken.
Freeze leftover chicken and thaw to make chicken cakes.

RÉMOULADE SAUCE

1 cup mayonnaise	1 tablespoon chopped parsley
3 green onions, sliced	¼ teaspoon cayenne pepper
2 tablespoons Creole mustard	1-2 tablespoons chili sauce
2 garlic cloves, minced	

RÉMOULADE SAUCE

Blend mayonnaise, green onions, mustard, garlic, parsley, cayenne, and chili sauce until smooth. Set aside.

CHICKEN CAKES

2 tablespoons margarine	1 cup bread crumbs
1 medium sweet red pepper, diced	1 large egg, slightly beaten
4 green onions, thinly sliced	2 tablespoons mayonnaise
2 teaspoons garlic	1 tablespoon Creole mustard
4 cups cooked chopped chicken	2 teaspoons Creole seasoning
	¼ cup vegetable oil

CHICKEN CAKES

Melt margarine in a large skillet over medium heat. Sauté pepper, green onion, and garlic 3-4 minutes or until tender. Combine pepper mixture, chicken, bread crumbs, egg, mayonnaise, mustard, and seasoning. Mix well. Shape mixture into 8 patties. Heat 2 tablespoons oil in a large skillet over medium heat. Cook patties for 3 minutes per side until golden browned. Drain on paper towels. Add more oil while frying. Serve immediately with Rémoulade Sauce.

YIELD: 8 SERVINGS

Rémoulade is a classic French sauce composed of mayonnaise and mustard. In France, they add capers, gherkins, herbs, and anchovies. When this sauce was brought to Louisiana, it became Southern style Remoulade sauce, which has cayenne pepper and chili sauce! As we like it — with a bit of heat!

CURRIED FRIED WONTONS

Perfect paired with cocktails.

5	tablespoons vegetable oil, divided	1	tablespoon curry powder
1	pound ground beef or veal	1	potato, cooked and mashed
2	tablespoons soy sauce	1	pound wonton wrappers
½	teaspoon kosher salt	2	cups vegetable oil
1½	teaspoons sugar		
1	cup minced onion		

Heat skillet until hot. Add 4 tablespoons oil. Stir fry beef until crumbled. Add soy sauce, salt, and sugar. Stir well and transfer to a bowl.

Reheat skillet and add 1 tablespoon oil. Sauté onion until translucent. Add curry and sauté 1 minute until well blended. Return meat mixture to skillet. Add potato. Cook and stir until blended. Transfer to bowl to cool.

Cover wrappers with a damp cloth to prevent drying. Place a wrapper on counter with one corner pointing down. Place ¾ teaspoon filling on this corner. Roll corner over filling to form a roll about halfway up the wrapper. Moisten left corner with water and bring around the right corner. Stick on top of moistened corner. Press corner to seal. Cover finished wontons with damp cloth while filling remaining wontons.

Heat 2 cups oil in a deep skillet or Dutch oven. Drop 6 to 9 wontons in hot oil. Using a chopstick, allow wontons to float freely and turn frequently. Fry until lightly browned. Drain on paper towels.

YIELD: 12 SERVINGS

SALAMI NASCH

1	(2 pound) beef salami		1	(12 ounce) bottle chili sauce
½	teaspoon dried rosemary		¼	cup red or white wine
½	cup packed brown sugar		1	teaspoon spicy mustard
½	teaspoon Worcestershire sauce			

Trim salami ends and remove casing. Cut slits on bottom to avoid rolling. Score 2 to 3 crisscross slits on top. Place in a baking dish. Blend rosemary, brown sugar, Worcestershire sauce, chili sauce, wine, and mustard. Pour sauce over salami. Bake at 350 degrees for 1 hour, basting every 15 minutes. Serve salami on a cutting board or slice into ½-inch pieces and cut into quarters. Serve with toothpicks.

YIELD: 12 TO 15 SERVINGS

SALAMI SALAD

A deli favorite reconstructed as a spread.

1	pound salami, ground		1	tablespoon deli mustard
3	hard-boiled eggs, ground			Mayonnaise to moisten
½	cup sweet relish			Assorted crackers

Blend salami, eggs, relish, mustard, and enough mayonnaise to bind mixture. Serve with crackers.

YIELD: 8 TO 10 SERVINGS

Place a scoop of Salami Salad and a scoop of Eggs and Caramelized Onion Salad on a bed of lettuce to serve as an appetizer.

NOT THE USUAL PIGS IN A BLANKET

This crowd pleaser appeals to young and old alike!

SPICY ONION SPREAD

2	cups finely chopped onions		Pinch of cayenne pepper
1	tablespoon vegetable oil	2	tablespoons sugar
½	teaspoon kosher salt	1	tablespoon vinegar
¼	teaspoon pepper	¼	teaspoon dried thyme

SPICY ONION SPREAD

Sauté onions in hot oil in a skillet with salt, pepper, and cayenne 7-9 minutes or until golden browned. Add sugar and cook an additional 1-2 minutes. Stir in vinegar and thyme. Cook for 1 minute. Remove from heat and cool. May prepare in advance and refrigerate in an airtight container for up to 1 week.

PIGS IN A BLANKET

1	large egg, slightly beaten	1	cup spicy onion spread
2	tablespoons water	2	pounds beef sausage, cut into 18 pieces
	Puff pastry sheets		Creole seasoning

PIGS IN A BLANKET

Preheat oven to 375 degrees. Whisk together egg and water. Set aside. Roll out puff pastry to ¼-inch thickness. Cut into 18 pieces. Spoon 1 tablespoon Spicy Onion Spread in center of dough. Place sausage piece onto spread. Roll pastry around sausage covering completely. Place on a parchment paper-lined baking sheet. Cover baking sheet with plastic wrap and set aside for 30 minutes.

Brush egg mixture on tops and sides of pastry. Sprinkle with Creole seasoning. Bake at 375 degrees for 30 minutes or until golden browned. Cool slightly.

YIELD: 8 SERVINGS

May prepare pigs in advance and freeze before baking. Thaw and bake as directed.

TUNA TARTARE

½ pound ahi tuna, small diced	½ teaspoon sesame oil
½ cup minced green onions	¼ cup soy sauce
1 teaspoon minced ginger	Dash of lime juice
1 teaspoon wasabi paste	Toasted baguettes

Combine tuna, green onion, ginger, wasabi, oil, soy sauce, and lime juice. Mix well. Adjust soy sauce and lime juice to taste. Serve with toasted baguettes.

YIELD: 4 SERVINGS

Place mixture in a 4 to 5 inch metal cookie cutter to form a mold. Unmold just before serving.

CAVIAR PIE

6 hard-boiled eggs, peeled and chopped	⅔ cup sour cream
3 tablespoons mayonnaise	4 ounces caviar, drained and chilled
1 small red onion, minced	Chopped parsley and lemon wedges for garnish (optional)
1 (8 ounce) package cream cheese, softened	Pumpernickel or unsalted crackers

Combine eggs and mayonnaise. Spread evenly in a greased 8-inch springform pan. Sprinkle red onion on top. Blend cream cheese and sour cream. Using a wet spatula, spread cream cheese mixture over onion. Cover and refrigerate for 3 hours or overnight.

Before serving, spread caviar evenly to edges. Loosen pan and lift off sides. Garnish with parsley and lemon wedges. Serve with pumpernickel or unsalted crackers.

YIELD: 10 TO 12 SERVINGS

This dish is quite impressive to serve to special guests and yet so simple to put together. Lightly rinsing the caviar and allowing it to drain will help spread the caviar.

TUNA IN A PUFF PASTRY WITH SAUCE

SAUCE

4	tablespoons butter or margarine	2	tablespoons beef flavored soup base
¼	cup all-purpose flour	¼	teaspoon garlic powder
3	cups water	1	tablespoon soy sauce

SAUCE

Melt butter or margarine in saucepan. Stir in flour until browned. Add water. Cook and stir until smooth and thickened. Add soup base, garlic powder, and soy sauce. Cook until smooth and thickened.

TUNA

2	tablespoons butter or margarine	1	egg, beaten
1	onion, chopped	1	(15 ounce) can small peas, drained
2	stalks celery, chopped	1	(12 ounce) can tuna packed in water, drained
8	ounces mushrooms, chopped	2	puff pastry sheets

TUNA

Preheat oven to 350 degrees. Melt butter or margarine in a skillet. Sauté onion, celery, and mushroom until soft. Transfer to a bowl. Add egg, peas, and tuna. Place one pastry sheet on a greased non-stick baking sheet. Spread tuna mixture over pastry. Place second pastry sheet on top. Bake at 350 degrees for 45 minutes or until pastry is browned and crispy. Cut pastry into 18 triangles. Top each triangle with sauce.

YIELD: 8 SERVINGS

Don't bother making puff pastry yourself! Save your time for something else. You can get puff pastry sheets in the freezer section of your grocery. The puff pastry needs a little time to thaw so that you can more easily roll it out and cut it up.

SIMPLE PÂTÉ TUNA APPETIZER

A reliable simple hors d'oerves that everyone will request.

1   (8 ounce) package cream cheese, softened
2   tablespoons chili sauce
2   teaspoons minced parsley
1   teaspoon minced onion
½   teaspoon hot pepper sauce
2   (6½ ounce) cans tuna in water, drained
    Crackers or pita chips

Combine cream cheese, chili sauce, parsley, onion, pepper sauce, and tuna. Mix well until smooth. Pour mixture into favorite mold. Refrigerate. Unmold and serve with crackers or pita chips.

YIELD: 6 TO 8 SERVINGS

SESAME CRAB "NOODLES"

4-6 garlic cloves, minced
⅓   cup sugar
⅓   cup wine vinegar
⅓   cup soy sauce
⅓   cup vegetable oil
1   teaspoon hot Chinese chili sauce
2   packages imitation crab sticks
4   green onions, chopped
2   teaspoons sesame seeds, toasted

Combine garlic, sugar, vinegar, soy sauce, oil, and chili sauce in a saucepan. Bring to boil. Cut each crab stick in half, then cut each half into 4 strips. Add crab to sauce and cook until crab shreds, looking like noodles. Sprinkle with green onions and sesame seeds.

YIELD: 4 TO 6 SERVINGS

Serve warm over a bed of rice or serve cool.

FISH CAKES

DIPPING SAUCE

1 cup mayonnaise	1½-2 tablespoons Dijon mustard
1 tablespoon capers	½ tablespoon Cajun seasoning
2 stalks celery, minced	Cayenne pepper to taste (optional)

DIPPING SAUCE

Place mayonnaise, capers, celery, mustard, seasoning, and cayenne in a food processor. Process until smooth.

FISH CAKES

1 (1½ pound) fresh cod fillet
¼ cup mayonnaise
½ teaspoon Creole or Cajun spices
¾ cup panko crumbs

FISH CAKES

Bake cod at 350 degrees for 15-18 minutes. Drain and flake well. Combine fish with mayonnaise and spices. Shape mixture into small 1-2 inch high patties. Coat in panko crumbs. Place on a baking sheet. Bake at 350 degrees for 15 minutes or until browned and firm. Flip and bake an additional 10 minutes. Spread sauce on serving plate. Place fish cakes on top and garnish with red pepper and/or fresh herbs.

YIELD: 6 SERVINGS

CHEDDAR RING

The Yankees will love this Southern treasure!

1 pound grated Cheddar cheese	1 garlic clove, minced
1 cup chopped pecans	½ teaspoon Tabasco sauce
¾ cup mayonnaise	1 cup strawberry preserves
1 small onion, grated	Assorted crackers

Combine Cheddar cheese, pecans, mayonnaise, onion, garlic, and Tabasco. Mix well. Spoon mixture into a ring mold, lined with plastic wrap. Refrigerate. When ready to serve, unmold onto a platter and top with preserves. Serve with crackers.

YIELD: 6 TO 8 SERVINGS

CREAMY MUSHROOMS

The aroma of this cooking will drive up your appetite!

1	stick butter	½	teaspoon dried thyme
1	tablespoon minced garlic	½	teaspoon dried oregano
1	tablespoon red wine	2	cups whipping cream
2	teaspoons soy sauce	3	pounds whole button mushrooms
½	teaspoon seasoned salt		

Melt butter in a saucepan. Add garlic, wine, soy sauce, seasoned salt, thyme, and oregano. Cook over medium heat 2-3 minutes until flavors are released and wine is reduced. Add cream and cook until thickened. Stir in mushrooms. Moisture will release from mushrooms. Cook until mushrooms are tender and sauce is reduced again. Serve in small individual bowls or martini glasses.

YIELD: 6 SERVINGS

This is also delicious as a sauce over pasta.

Reducing means boiling a liquid rapidly until the volume is reduced by moisture evaporation. The result is a stock, sauce or wine, which is thicker with a more intense flavor. It is best to season the sauce after the reduction because the flavor can be powerful.

VIDALIA ONION DIP

These onions are named for the town of Vidalia, Georgia, where they are grown. They are exceedingly sweet and juicy.

1	(8 ounce) package cream cheese, softened	1½	teaspoons Worcestershire sauce
1-2	tablespoons mayonnaise		Dash of Tabasco sauce
1	large Vidalia or sweet onion, finely chopped	1	cup grated Parmesan cheese

Blend cream cheese, mayonnaise, onion, Worcestershire sauce, Tabasco, and Parmesan cheese. Mix well. Spoon mixture into a casserole dish. Bake at 350 degrees for 25-30 minutes.

YIELD: 6 SERVINGS

CHILE CON QUESO

½ pound fresh roasted poblano peppers
2 tablespoons vegetable oil
1 cup chopped onions
¼ teaspoon cayenne pepper
2 tablespoons all-purpose flour

1 large tomato, chopped
1 cup cream
1½ cups grated or shredded Cheddar cheese
1 cup shredded Monterey Jack cheese
   Tortilla chips

Broil peppers on a baking sheet, turning once, for 7-10 minutes until all sides are charred black. Transfer peppers to a paper bag and cool for 15 minutes. Peel off skins, cut in half and discard seeds and stems. Chop peppers and set aside.

Heat oil in large stockpot. Sauté onion and cayenne 6 minutes or until very tender. Stir in flour 1-2 minutes until thickened. Add tomatoes and reserved peppers. Cook for 1 minute. Slowly add cream. Cook and stir 3-4 minutes until thickened. Add Cheddar and Jack cheese and stir until cheese melts. Serve warm with chips.

YIELD: 6 TO 8 SERVINGS

May roast a batch of poblano peppers and freeze them in zip-top plastic bags-then making this dish becomes a snap!

DIXIE HEARTS OF ARTICHOKE DIP

The mozzarella cheese added to this dish gives it that extra gooey cheesy texture!

2 (14 ounce) cans artichoke hearts, chopped
1 (8 ounce) package shredded mozzarella cheese
1¼ cups shredded Parmesan cheese

½ cup mayonnaise
   Dash of garlic salt
   Bread crumbs
   Butter pats

Combine artichoke, mozzarella cheese, Parmesan cheese, mayonnaise, and garlic salt. Spoon mixture into a casserole dish. Top with bread crumbs. Dot with butter pats. Bake at 350 degrees for 35 minutes.

YIELD: 6 SERVINGS

MEDITERRANEAN DIP

*This is one of those dips which you can usually
find all the ingredients in your cabinet or refrigerator.*

1 (8 ounce) package cream cheese, softened
1 medium onion, diced
1 cup plus ⅓ cup grated Parmesan cheese, divided
½ cup mayonnaise

½ cup plus ¼ cup sun-dried tomatoes packed in oil, drained, divided
2 tablespoons capers, rinsed
¼ cup chopped black olives
1 teaspoon minced garlic
½ teaspoon dried rosemary
¼ teaspoon pepper

Preheat oven to 350 degrees. Combine cream cheese, onion, 1 cup Parmesan cheese, mayonnaise, ½ cup sun-dried tomatoes, capers, black olives, garlic, rosemary, and pepper. Mix well. Spoon mixture into a 9-inch pie plate. Top with ⅓ cup Parmesan cheese and ¼ cup sun-dried tomatoes. Bake at 350 degrees for 15 minutes or until hot and bubbly.

YIELD: 8 SERVINGS

It is good to have ingredients on hand to make dips. Some of the staples to keep in your refrigerator or cabinet are sour cream, mayonnaise, cream cheese, cheeses, capers, artichokes, sundried tomatoes, garlic, olives, onions and a variety of spices! From these you can make dips that will WOW your guests.

FANCY LAYERED DIP

This dip was served at a brunch with a lot of Northerners-they are still talking about it!

2 (8 ounce) packages cream cheese, softened
2 (4 ounce) jars pesto
2 (16 ounce) cans hearts of palm, sliced

2 (15 ounce) cans artichoke hearts, chopped
1 (4 ounce) jar sun-dried tomatoes in oil, drained and sliced
1 (4 ounce) package crumbled feta cheese

Layer the cream cheese, pesto, hearts of palm, artichoke, tomatoes, and feta cheese in a casserole dish. Bake at 350 degrees for 15-20 minutes.

YIELD: 12 TO 15 SERVINGS

ARTICHOKE MUSHROOM DIP

1   stick margarine or ½ cup vegetable oil

¼   cup all-purpose flour

1   onion, finely chopped

2   garlic cloves, chopped

½   teaspoon dried thyme

1   (4 ounce) can sliced or chopped mushrooms, reserving liquid

½   teaspoon browning sauce

½   teaspoon chopped parsley

Salt and pepper to taste

1   (14 ounce) can artichoke quarters, chopped

French bread or onion party toasts

Melt margarine or oil in saucepan. Stir in flour until browned. Sauté onion and garlic until tender. Add thyme, mushrooms, ½ cup mushroom liquid, browning sauce, parsley, salt, pepper, and artichokes. Cook and stir for 10 minutes. Spoon mixture into a small round serving dish. Heat in oven until ready to serve with French bread or onion party toasts.

YIELD: 8 SERVINGS

ONION PARTY TOASTS

1 onion, chopped

1 cup mayonnaise

¼ cup shredded Cheddar cheese (optional)

1 loaf party rye bread

Paprika for garnish

Combine onion, mayonnaise, and Cheddar cheese. Spread mixture over bread. Sprinkle with paprika. Place on baking sheet. Broil until bubbly.

CHESTER'S DIP

1   (8 ounce) container sour cream

8   ounces mayonnaise

1   small can water chestnuts, drained and chopped

5   green onions, chopped

2   teaspoons soy sauce (low-sodium is perfectly fine)

Mix all ingredients. Chill a minimum of 2 or 3 hours before serving. Serve with tortilla chips. Also great with raw veggies.

Water chestnuts are sold already chopped wich makes this easy dip even easier!

SPINACH DIP

2   (10 ounce) packages frozen chopped spinach, thawed
1¼ cups chopped onions
3   tablespoons butter
1   (8 ounce) package cream cheese, softened
1   (14 ounce) can artichoke hearts, drained and chopped

½-¾ cup whipping cream
1½   cups grated Parmesan cheese plus more for topping
1   tablespoon garlic powder
     Salt and pepper to taste
     Tortilla chips, sour cream, salsa or *Don Pepino* pizza sauce

Cook spinach according to package directions. Drain well and set aside. Sauté onion in butter until golden browned. Add cream cheese. Stir until cream cheese melts. Slowly stir in spinach, artichoke, cream, Parmesan cheese, garlic powder, salt, and pepper. Spoon mixture into a casserole dish. Top with Parmesan cheese. Broil for 2-3 minutes. Serve with tortilla chips, sour cream, salsa, or pizza sauce.

YIELD: 12 SERVINGS

PIMENTO CHEESE SPREAD

This traditional Southern dip can be spread on sandwiches.
For a warm version, bake mixture in a 2-quart casserole dish at
350 degrees 20 minutes or until golden browned and bubbly.

1   cup mayonnaise
1   (4 ounce) jar diced pimentos, drained
1   teaspoon Worcestershire sauce
1   teaspoon finely grated onion
¼   teaspoon cayenne pepper

1   (8 ounce) block extra sharp Cheddar cheese, finely shredded
1   (8 ounce) block sharp Cheddar cheese, shredded
    Assorted crackers

Combine mayonnaise, pimentos, Worcestershire sauce, onion, and cayenne. Stir in Cheddar cheeses. Mix well. Serve with crackers. Store in refrigerator for up to 1 week.

YIELD: 15 SERVINGS

MARINATED CHEESE CUBES

You are having a crowd-usually you just throw out some sliced cheese or chunk of cheese. Make this the night before and you have something beautiful to serve and great to eat. It looks fancy, but it is not!

½	cup olive oil	½	teaspoon salt
½	cup white wine vinegar	½	teaspoon pepper
¼	cup fresh lime juice	1	(8 ounce) block sharp Cheddar cheese, chilled
½	(7½ ounce) jar roasted sweet red peppers, drained and diced	1	(8 ounce) block Monterey Jack cheese with peppers, chilled
3	green onions, minced	1	(8 ounce) package cream cheese, chilled
3	tablespoons chopped parsley		Assorted crackers
3	tablespoons chopped cilantro		
1	teaspoon sugar		

Whisk together oil, vinegar, and lime juice until blended. Stir in peppers, green onion, parsley, cilantro, sugar, salt, and pepper. Cube Cheddar cheese, Jack cheese, and cream cheese. Place in a shallow dish. Pour marinade over cheeses. Cover and refrigerate for 8 hours. Transfer marinated cheese to a large glass jar or serving dish. Spoon marinade over top. Serve with crackers.

YIELD: 15 TO 20 SERVINGS

THE SOUTH'S BEST DIP

3	packages frozen avocados	3	bunches scallions, chopped
2	cups mayonnaise		Black olives, optional
1	cup sour cream	1	(8 ounce) package shredded Cheddar cheese
1	package taco seasoning		
3	tomatoes, chopped		

Spread avocados on a platter. Mix together mayonnaise, sour cream, taco seasoning, and spread over the avocados. Add chopped tomatoes, scallions, and olives on top. Spread cheese on top and serve with chips or crackers.

This is ALWAYS a crowd pleaser with children and adults.

BASIL AND SUN-DRIED TOMATO TORTA

This is beautiful! Top with a few chopped sun-dried tomatoes, pine nuts or chopped basil leaves. This is a most impressive appetizer. Visually it is beautiful and very professional looking. It tastes amazing.

½   pound thinly sliced provolone cheese

2   (8 ounce) packages cream cheese, softened

½   cup pesto

2   garlic cloves, minced

2   (4 ounce) jars sun-dried tomatoes in oil, drained and coarsely chopped

Plain toasted baguettes slices

Line an 8 or 9-inch pie plate with plastic wrap, with overhanging edges. Arrange overlapping layers of provolone cheese on bottom and up sides of plate. Blend cream cheese, pesto, and garlic. Spread one-third mixture over cheese. Top with a layer of tomatoes. Repeat with a layer of cream cheese mixture and tomatoes. Top with remaining cream cheese mixture using a wet spatula. Fold plastic wrap over top and pat down top. Refrigerate for 6-8 hours. When ready to serve, pull back top plastic wrap. Invert plate onto a platter. Lift off pan and lift off bottom plastic wrap. Serve with plain toasted baguettes slices.

YIELD: 8 TO 10 SERVINGS

HOT PIZZA DIP

1   (8 ounce) package cream cheese, softened

1   teaspoon Italian seasoning

1   teaspoon garlic powder

1   (8 ounce) package shredded mozzarella cheese

1   (8 ounce) package shredded Cheddar cheese

½   cup *DonPepino* pizza sauce

Tortilla chips

Combine cream cheese, Italian seasoning, and garlic powder. Spread mixture on bottom of greased 9-inch pie plate. Combine mozzarella cheese and Cheddar cheese. Sprinkle half over cream cheese layer. Top with pizza sauce. Sprinkle with remaining cheese mixture. Bake at 350 degrees for 20-30 minutes. Serve warm with tortilla chips.

YIELD: 8 SERVINGS

Soups & Sandwiches

Sponsored by Rochelle and Ed Wiener
In honor of our chef and our daughter,
Tracy Rapp
She has given her time and energy to this labor of love, "The Cookbook."

On any given day in 1945, lunchtime at Rosen's Kosher

Delicatessen was quite a scene. Everyone felt at home in Rosen's; they came to socialize, relax and, of course, sample Rosen's famous soups, homemade corned beef and sweet and sour short ribs, a recipe that is included in this cookbook. From local politicians to the kosher Jewish community in Memphis and the small Jewish communities scattered throughout Arkansas and Mississippi, eating at Rosen's was like eating with family.

Rochelle Goldstein Wiener's parents, Fannie and Sam Goldstein, owned and operated Rosen's, originally established by Fannie's parents in the early 1900's. Rochelle recalls it was the local place to meet for business or to talk politics. It was also where she met her husband, Ed Wiener, who came to Rosen's looking for a taste of home. "Where does a nice Jewish boy from Brooklyn find a good corned beef sandwich in Memphis, Tennessee?" He stayed to visit with Rochelle, eventually marrying her and settling in Memphis.

After the family hired a baker from the famous Junior's bakery in Brooklyn, Rosen's began supplying the Jewish community with bagels, bialys, cheesecakes, and pastries. Rosen's was one of the first kosher caterers in Memphis. They once catered a party at the Baron Hirsch Synagogue attended by 1000 people in honor of Eleanor Roosevelt. Fannie was known as a caterer who served food that was not only delicious, it was also presented with artistic flair.

Yet Rosen's was not the only kosher deli in town. Halpern's, another family-run deli in midtown Memphis, was owned and operated by Thelma and Louis Halpern until 1982. Halpern's originally served three meals a day through the end of World War II, closing only for the Sabbath. Thelma and Louis' son Gil recalls that Sunday was the day to be at Halpern's. People came to visit with Thelma and eat her delicious mushroom barley soup and her chili that was once voted best in Memphis. Gil spent many days counting hundreds of bagels they bought from the local kosher bakery to serve to their customers.

Rosen's Deli and Halpern's Deli had what Southerners like to call a "friendly competition". The families were best of friends and shared both customers and ideas. They embodied a spirit of warmth and hominess that became synonymous with Memphis' Jewish community. Memphis' long tradition of fine kosher food owes much to these two pioneering families.

34

CREAMY PARMESAN TOMATO SOUP

This recipe was inspired by an Italian lady that made fresh mozzarella and creamy Parmesan soup in her tiny New York City basement.

Olive oil
1 yellow or sweet onion
3 garlic cloves, minced
10 fresh tomatoes, quartered
1 (15 ounce) can diced plum tomatoes

2 cups heavy cream
5 cups parve chicken broth
4 slices bread, toasted
¾ cup grated Parmesan cheese
Salt and pepper to taste
1 tablespoon dried parsley

Heat oil in a stockpot over medium heat. Sauté onion and garlic until translucent. Add tomatoes, canned tomatoes, cream, and chicken soup base. Bring to boil. Reduce heat and simmer for 20-30 minutes. Add toast and Parmesan cheese. Purée soup in batches in a blender or with an immersion blender until smooth. Add salt and pepper. Top with parsley.

YIELD: 6 TO 8 SERVINGS

SEAFOOD CHOWDER

1 tablespoon vegetable oil
2 cups chopped onions
2 carrots, shredded
1 teaspoon minced garlic
¼ teaspoon crushed red pepper
4 cups parve chicken broth
4 Roma tomatoes, diced

2 potatoes, peeled and diced
1 cup heavy cream
2 (15 ounce) cans whole kernel corn, undrained
1 pound imitation crab
   Salt and pepper to taste
1 tablespoon chopped parsley

Heat oil in large stockpot over medium heat. Add onion, carrot, garlic, and red pepper. Sauté vegetables until tender. Add broth, tomatoes and potato. Bring to boil. Reduce heat and slowly stir in cream. Simmer for 15 minutes. Add corn, imitation crab, salt, and pepper. Simmer until thickened. Stir in parsley and serve.

YIELD: 6 TO 8 SERVINGS

May substitute non-dairy whipped topping and ½ cup soymilk for the heavy cream. Also may substitute 1 (14 ounce) can creamed corn for 1 can whole kernel corn.

SOUTHERN STYLE CORN BREAD

½ cup cooking oil, divided

2 beaten eggs

1 cup non-dairy sour cream

1 cup creamed corn

½ teaspoon salt

1 cup self-rising cornmeal

Preheat oven to 400 degrees. Put ¼ cup oil in a 10-inch ovensafe skillet. Place the skillet in the oven while it is preheating to heat the oil. In a separate bowl, combine the egs, non-dairy sour cream, creamed corn, salt, cornmeal, and the remaining ¼ cup oil. Combine well, but do not over mix. Pour the batter in the hot skillet and bake for 30 minutes. Serve warm.

ARUGULA, LEEK AND POTATO SOUP

1	medium bunch leeks	1	bunch arugula
1	tablespoon unsalted margarine		Kosher salt and pepper to taste
1	tablespoon olive oil		Finely snipped chives for garnish
3	pounds red potatoes, cubed		
6	cups chicken broth		

Cut off bottoms and most of the green tops of leeks and discard. Discard tough outer leaves. Cube trimmed leeks. Place in a sieve and rinse under running cold water. Drain.

Heat margarine and oil in a large stockpot. Sauté leeks over low heat, stirring occasionally, until soft. Add potatoes and broth. Bring to boil. Reduce heat, cover and simmer until potatoes are tender. Discard lower halves of arugula stems. Rinse and shake off excess water. Add arugula to soup and cook until wilted. Cool slightly. Purée soup in batches in a blender. Return to stockpot and heat thoroughly. Add salt and pepper. Garnish with chives.

YIELD: 8 TO 10 SERVINGS

Keep the potato skins on to make the soup have red flecks and a heartier taste.

SWEET POTATO-PEANUT SOUP

This rich Southern soup packs some super flavors—peanuts and sweet potatoes!

1	tablespoon margarine	1½	pounds sweet potatoes, peeled and cubed
½	large sweet onion, chopped	3¼	cups chicken broth
1	small stalk celery, diced	1	cup soymilk
2	carrots, sliced	½	cup creamy peanut butter
¼	teaspoon cayenne pepper		Chopped toasted peanuts

Melt margarine in a large Dutch oven. Sauté onion, celery, carrot, and cayenne over medium heat for 3 minutes. Add sweet potatoes and chicken broth. Cook, stirring occasionally, for 30 minutes. Purée soup in batches in a blender or food processor until smooth. Return to Dutch oven. Whisk in soymilk and peanut butter. Simmer, stirring often, for 15 minutes. Garnish with toasted peanuts.

YIELD: 4 SERVINGS

ROASTED CARROT GINGER SOUP

There are many ways to store ginger: Cover any leftover ginger with dry sherry and store in the refrigerator in a small glass jar. It will be usable for a year.

Wrap ginger in a paper towel and place in a zip-top plastic bag.
Store in the vegetable bin in refrigerator.

John, our produce man in Memphis, says you can even freeze it!

1½ pounds carrots, peeled and chopped

1 pound parsnips, peeled and chopped

1 large onion, sliced

3 inch piece ginger, peeled and chopped

6 tablespoons margarine

3 tablespoons packed dark brown sugar

8 cups chicken broth

Salt to taste

¼ cup soymilk

Preheat oven to 350 degrees. Combine carrot, parsnip, onion, and ginger in a shallow roasting pan. Dot with margarine. Sprinkle with brown sugar. Bake at 350 degrees for 2 hours until very tender.

Transfer vegetables to stockpot. Add broth and salt. Bring to boil. Reduce heat and simmer, partially covered, for 10 minutes.

Purée soup in batches in blender or food processor, adding more broth if necessary. Return soup to pot. Heat thoroughly. Stir in soymilk.

YIELD: 6 SERVINGS

BUTTERNUT SQUASH SOUP

This Autumn treat is a Sukkot tradition for one Memphis family.
They invite you to make it one of yours!

2   tablespoons margarine
2   large shallots, finely chopped
2   medium stalks celery, chopped
3   pounds butternut squash, peeled, seeded and cut into chunks

1   pound parsnips, peeled and cut into chunks (optional)
1   medium Granny Smith apple, peeled and cut into chunks
4   (15 ounce) cans chicken broth or homemade broth

Melt margarine over medium heat. Add shallots and celery. Cover and cook 5 minutes or until softened. Stir in squash, parsnips, and apples. Add 2 cans broth. Cover and bring to boil. Reduce heat, cover and simmer 20 minutes or until vegetables are tender. Purée soup in batches in the blender until smooth. Return to pot. Add remaining 2 cans broth. Heat thoroughly.

YIELD: 8 SERVINGS

TOMATO SOUP WITH ISRAELI COUSCOUS

This is as much a meal as it is a soup! And Israelis love their tomatoes too!

4	tablespoons olive oil	12½	cups vegetable or chicken broth
4	onions, chopped	½	package Israeli couscous
3-4	carrots, diced	4-5	mint sprigs, chopped
2	(15 ounce) cans *DonPepino* pizza sauce	½	teaspoon ground cumin
12	tomatoes, roughly chopped	½	bunch fresh cilantro or 5 sprigs, chopped
2	teaspoons chopped garlic, divided		Cayenne pepper, salt and black pepper to taste

Heat oil in a large stockpot. Sauté onion and carrot for 10 minutes until soft. Add pizza sauce, tomatoes, half garlic, broth, couscous, mint, cumin, cilantro, cayenne, salt, and pepper. Bring to boil. Add remaining garlic. Reduce heat and simmer 7-10 minutes, stirring occasionally, until couscous is tender. Ladle into bowls and serve hot.

YIELD: 4 TO 6 SERVINGS

CAULIFLOWER WHITE WINTER SOUP

Creamy white with the comfort of winter!
Roasting the vegetables gives this soup depth of flavor!

1	whole cauliflower, trimmed and cut up	2	parsnips, peeled and diced
2	medium leeks, mostly white part, finely chopped	2	garlic cloves, minced
		⅓	cup olive oil
1	stalk celery, trimmed and diced	6-8	cups chicken broth
			Salt and pepper to taste

Preheat oven to 350 degrees. Combine cauliflower, leeks, celery, parsnip, garlic, and oil in a shallow roasting pan. Roast at 350 degrees for 1 hour, 30 minutes, stirring every 30 minutes. Transfer to a stockpot. Add enough broth to cover vegetables. Simmer for 20 minutes. Cool. Purée with an immersion blender. Reheat and add salt and pepper.

YIELD: 6 SERVINGS

CORN CHOWDER

Puréed corn creates creaminess.

1	tablespoon vegetable oil	1	teaspoon dried rosemary
2	cups chopped onion	1	teaspoon dried thyme
8	(15 ounce) cans whole kernel corn, divided	¼	teaspoon pepper
			Cayenne pepper to taste
6	cups chicken broth, divided	2	tablespoons chopped basil
1	cup diced sweet red pepper		

Heat oil in large stockpot. Sauté onion 5 minutes or until translucent. Add 5 cans corn and sauté an additional 5 minutes. Pour in 4 cups chicken broth. Cook for 30 minutes. Purée soup in batches in a blender until smooth. Return to pot. Add red pepper, rosemary, thyme, pepper, cayenne, remaining 3 cans corn and 2 cups chicken broth. Cook and stir over low heat for 20 minutes. Stir in basil. Be careful to not scorch bottom.

YIELD: 8 TO 10 SERVINGS

May use fresh corn to get that off-the-cob flavor.

FRESH TOMATO SOUP WITH RICE

*Rich ripe tomatoes and a hint of saffron sing in your
mouth with every bite of this French country-style soup.*

2   pounds tomatoes
2   medium onions, halved lengthwise
    and thinly sliced crosswise
1   medium carrot, coarsely grated
1   stalk celery, finely chopped
4   large garlic cloves, chopped
3   (3 x 1-inch) strips orange zest,
    finely chopped
1   teaspoon finely chopped thyme
¼   teaspoon dried hot red pepper
¼   teaspoon fennel seeds
1   bay leaf
3   tablespoons extra virgin
    olive oil

2   tablespoons tomato paste
3   cups water
1¾ cups reduced sodium
    chicken broth
¾   teaspoon salt
¼   teaspoon pepper
1   pinch saffron threads, crumbled
1-2 teaspoons sugar, divided
¼   cup long grain rice
2   tablespoons chopped flat
    leaf parsley
¼   cup chopped basil
    Salt to taste

Cut a shallow X in bottom of each tomato. Blanch tomatoes in batches of 2-3 in a 6-quart pot of boiling water for 10 seconds. Transfer with a slotted spoon to a bowl of ice cold water.

Peel tomatoes and cut in half crosswise. Squeeze halves gently, cut side down, over a sieve set over a bowl to extract seeds and reserve juice. Press on seeds and discard. Reserve juice and tomatoes.

In a 3-quart heavy stockpot, cook onion, carrot, celery, garlic, zest, thyme, red pepper, fennel seeds, and bay leaf in oil 5 minutes until tender. Add tomatoes, reserved juice, tomato paste, water, chicken broth, salt, pepper, saffron, and 1 teaspoon sugar. Simmer, uncovered, for 20 minutes breaking up tomatoes. Stir in rice. Simmer 10-20 minutes until rice is tender. Discard bay leaf. Stir in parsley, basil, 1 teaspoon sugar, and salt.

YIELD: 8 SERVINGS

Sometimes recipes seem complicated because they have a lot of ingredients. However, just gathering the ingredients is the hard part — particularly with soups. Don't let this list of ingredients stop you from giving this soup a chance — it is light and satisfying at the same time. It is great to make when the tomatoes are in season and freeze for a later date — like in the middle of winter when you are reminiscing about those abundant fresh tomatoes!

PUMPKIN AND COCONUT SOUP

This soup is best made with fresh pie pumpkins that are usually found during pumpkin season—September and October.

2 pounds 4 ounces pumpkin	1 small red chili pepper, chopped
1 tablespoon peanut oil	3¾ cups chicken broth
1 tablespoon yellow mustard seeds	5 tablespoons coconut cream
1 garlic clove, crushed	Salt and pepper to taste
1 large onion, chopped	Chopped cilantro for garnish
1 stalk celery, chopped	

Halve pumpkin and remove seeds. Cut away the skin, dice the flesh and reserve. Heat oil in a large stockpot. Fry mustard seeds until seeds begin to pop. Stir in garlic, onion, celery, and chili pepper. Stir-fry for 1-2 minutes.

Add reserved pumpkin flesh and chicken broth. Bring to boil. Reduce heat, cover and simmer 30 minutes or until vegetables are very tender. Purée soup in batches in blender or food processor until smooth. Return to pot. Stir in coconut cream. Add salt and pepper. Garnish with cilantro.

YIELD: 6 SERVINGS

Freeze this soup—you may get a hankering for it when the pumpkins are out of season!

When puréeing soups, you can use an immersion blender, a traditional blender or a food processor. First be sure to remove any sachets of herbs, bay leaves, bones, or other inedible ingredients. Allow soup to slightly cool. Fill the blender or processor half way to avoid overflow or scalding yourself. When using the immersion blender, keep the head of the blender completely submerged to prevent splattering. These techniques can provide a smooth, yet textured soup.

Soups & Sandwiches

LENTIL SOUP

A traditional winter warmer with Old Country origins.

3   cups lentils
2   quarts water
2   teaspoons salt
3   tablespoons olive oil
1½ cups chopped onion
1½ cups chopped sweet red pepper
4   carrots, chopped

1   (28 ounce) can whole peeled tomatoes
1   (16 ounce) can whole peeled tomatoes
1   (15 ounce) can *DonPepino* pizza sauce
Salt and pepper to taste

Combine lentils, water, and salt in a stockpot. Bring to boil. Cover, reduce heat and simmer for 30 minutes.

Heat oil in a large skillet. Sauté onion and pepper until tender. Add to stockpot. Stir in carrot, tomatoes, and pizza sauce. Cover and simmer for 30 minutes. Add salt and pepper.

YIELD: 4 TO 6 SERVINGS

LEMON ASPARAGUS SOUP

A fresh elegant springtime favorite!

2   pounds asparagus, chopped
2   cups chopped celery
6   cups chicken broth
1   teaspoon lemon zest

¼   cup lemon juice
⅛   teaspoon white pepper
1   cup parve whipping cream

Combine asparagus, celery, and broth in a stockpot. Bring to boil. Reduce heat and simmer for 20 minutes. Cool.

Purée soup in batches in blender until smooth. Return to pot. Stir in lemon zest, lemon juice, pepper, and whipping cream. Heat thoroughly but do not boil. Serve hot or cold.

YIELD: 4 SERVINGS

SOUTHERN SUMMER BERRY SOUP

This recipe is even better when made the day before and frozen.
May serve slushy. May prepare during the summer months when fresh
berries are in season, then freeze it for use later in the year.

1   pound fresh or 1 (20 ounce) package frozen strawberries or raspberries

2   cups water

½   cup sugar

1   tablespoon lemon juice
    Mint leaves, whipped cream, strawberries/raspberries for garnish

Purée strawberries, water, and sugar in a food processor until smooth. Add lemon juice. Serve chilled. Garnish with mint, whipped cream, strawberries/raspberries. Top with Apple Croutons.

YIELD: 2 TO 4 SERVINGS

APPLE CROUTONS

1 cup water

½ teaspoon lemon juice

1 Granny Smith apple, peeled and chopped

1½ cups flour

¾ teaspoon baking powder

½ teaspoon baking soda

½ teaspoon cinnamon

¼ teaspoon salt

¼ pound margarine

1 cup sugar

2 eggs

1 teaspoon vanilla

Lightly coat loaf pan with non-stick cooking spray. Add 1 cup of water with lemon juice and add apple to bowl. Mix flour, baking powder, baking soda, cinnamon, and salt. Beat margarine and sugar for 2 minutes on high. Add eggs one at a time. Add vanilla and beat another minute. Rinse and drain apples and add apples to batter. Beat 1 minute. Add dry ingredients, mix on low for 30 seconds. Pour into loaf pan. Bake for 45 minutes at 350 degrees. Allow to cool. Remove from pan and slice into cubes. Toast on cookie sheet for 15-20 minutes until toasty.

BLACK BEAN SOUP

Chicken and black beans pack protein into this Cuban classic.

1 medium onion, chopped
4 garlic cloves, minced
5 (16 ounce) cans black beans, drained and divided
2 (15 ounce) cans chicken broth
1 tablespoon ground cumin

1 teaspoon cayenne pepper
2 cups salsa
2 tablespoons lime juice
2 boneless, skinless chicken breast halves, cubed

Sauté onion and garlic in a stockpot until translucent. Add 4 cans beans, broth, cumin, cayenne, salsa, and lime juice. Mash remaining can beans and add to soup. Add chicken. Simmer for 1 hour until chicken is thoroughly cooked.

YIELD: 4 TO 6 SERVINGS

Chicken and black beans pack protein into this Cuban classic.

SLOW COOKER TURKEY SPLIT PEA SOUP

1 piece Turkey Schawarma
2 quarts water
2 cups dry split peas
1 cup barley
1 onion, chopped

3 carrots, diced
3 stalks celery, diced
2 potatoes, diced
2 tablespoons chopped dill
1-2 tablespoons dry soup mix

Combine turkey, water, peas, barley, onion, carrot, celery, potato, dill, and soup mix in a crockpot. Cook on high for 2-3 hours. Add water to the top and cook on low overnight.

Remove turkey and pull meat from bone and chop. Return to soup, mix well and serve.

YIELD: 6 SERVINGS

SPLIT PEA SOUP

This recipe has been a favorite for generations in one Memphis family, whose ancestors brought it with them from the Old Country. This is a soak-it-up-with-bread-lick-the-bowl-clean soup! They may have invented cheesecloth but the nylon hose seems to work best!

14 cups water	6 carrots
3 cups dry split peas	2 parsnips
3-4 thick bone-in short ribs	2 large onions
4 garlic cloves, minced	6 stalks celery, chopped
2 tablespoons salt	½ bunch parsley

Combine water, peas, ribs, garlic, and salt in a stockpot. Slowly bring to boil. When peas begin to break down, simmer for 1 hour, stirring often.

Chop carrot, parsnip, and onion in a food processor. Add to soup. Simmer an additional 30 minutes. Add celery and place parsley in nylon hose. Add to soup and simmer an additional 30 minutes. Discard nylon hose with the parsley inside.

YIELD: 8 TO 10 SERVINGS

BEEF AND BARLEY SOUP

3 pounds short ribs or chuck roast	2 carrots, diced
1½ teaspoons salt	2 stalks celery, sliced
3½ quarts water	2 teaspoons vegetable oil
2 large onions, diced	1 cup barley
½ pound fresh mushrooms, thinly sliced	Pepper to taste

Combine beef, salt, and water in a stockpot. Bring to boil. In a skillet, sauté onion, mushrooms, carrot, and celery in oil until lightly browned. Add vegetables, barley, and pepper to pot. Cover and simmer 2 hours, 30 minutes or until meat is tender. Add salt and pepper.

YIELD: 10 SERVINGS

MEATBALL SOUP

This soup tastes better the longer you have it.

- ¼ cup olive oil
- 1 yellow onion, chopped
- 1 cup chopped celery
- 2 garlic cloves, chopped
- 2 (14½ ounce) cans whole tomatoes with juice
- 2 (14 ounce) cans beef broth
- ¼ cup tomato paste
- 2 teaspoons dried Italian seasoning, divided
- 2 pounds ground beef
- 4 large eggs, slightly beaten
- ½ cup Italian-style bread crumbs
- ½ teaspoon salt
- ½ cup small shape pasta
- 3 cups baby spinach (optional)

Heat stockpot over medium-high heat. Add oil. Sauté onion and celery until soft. Add garlic and cook for 1 minute. Add tomatoes with juice, broth, tomato paste, and 1 teaspoon seasoning. Bring to simmer.

In a bowl, combine beef, eggs, bread crumbs, 1 teaspoon seasoning, and salt until thoroughly mixed. Roll mixture into smooth balls. Carefully add meatballs to soup. Gently stir, being careful not to break up meatballs. Simmer 20 minutes or until meatballs are cooked. Add pasta and spinach to hot soup. Cook 15 minutes until pasta is cooked.

YIELD: 10 SERVINGS

CURRY MANGO TUNA WRAP

Very versatile and tasty!

- 2 (6 ounce) cans tuna in water, drained
- ¼ cup raisins (optional)
- ¼ cup chopped pecans (optional)
- ½ cup mayonnaise
- 1 tablespoon vinegar
- ¼ cup chopped fresh parsley or chives
- 2 tablespoons curry powder
- 2 tablespoons-½ cup mango chutney or sliced mangoes
- Tortilla wraps

Combine tuna, raisins, and pecans. Blend in mayonnaise, vinegar, parsley, curry, and mango chutney. Mix well. Spread mixture over wraps and roll up tightly. Cut into half for individuals or cut into 1-2 inch slices for appetizers.

YIELD: 4 SERVINGS

May serve mixture over bed of lettuce with chopped green apples. Substitute peaches when mangoes are not in season!

CURRIED BEEF SOUP

The curry in this soup is so low key, you may not know it is there.
But you will appreciate the full flavor of the soup!

1   tablespoon vegetable oil
1   medium onion, chopped
1   stalk celery, chopped
1   carrot, julienne cut
½   teaspoon dried thyme
¾   teaspoon curry powder
¾   teaspoon hot curry powder
2   tablespoons all-purpose flour
2   tablespoons honey
1   large apple, peeled, cored and
    chopped

2   quarts beef broth
1   pound small red potatoes, cleaned
    and cubed with
    skin on
1   teaspoon dried parsley
1-2 teaspoons salt
½   teaspoon pepper
1-2 pounds beef, cubed
1   cup soymilk

Heat oil in stockpot. Add onion, celery, carrot, and thyme. Cook and stir for 5 minutes until onions are slightly browned. Stir in curry powders, flour, and honey. Cook and stir for 5 additional minutes. Stir in apple. Slowly pour in 1 quart beef broth. Cook until smooth and thickened. Add remaining 1 quart beef broth, potatoes, parsley, salt, pepper, and beef. Bring to boil. Reduce heat and simmer 45 minutes until potatoes are tender and beef is cooked. Remove from heat and slowly stir in soymilk. To reheat leftover soup, bring to a slow simmer.

YIELD: 6 SERVINGS

MINI MATZO BALL GUMBO SOUP

*It does not have to be Passover to love matzo balls, and you
do not have to be in Louisiana to appreciate a good gumbo!*

1	pound sausage	1	tablespoon spicy seasoning
1	tablespoon olive oil	2-3	teaspoons Creole seasoning
1	onion, chopped	8	cups beef broth
1	bell pepper, chopped	1	matzo ball mix, prepared and refrigerated
1	sweet red pepper, chopped		
1	yellow pepper, chopped	1	(16 ounce) package frozen okra
2	garlic cloves, minced		

Sauté sausage in oil in a hot skillet. Remove sausage. Add onion, all peppers, and garlic. Sauté until tender. Return sausage and add spicy and Creole seasoning. Pour in broth. Bring to boil.

Shape 1 teaspoon matzo mixture into balls and drop into soup. Cover and simmer for 15-20 minutes. Remove matzo balls. Add frozen okra and simmer for 15-20 minutes. Return matzo balls to soup.

YIELD: 8 TO 10 SERVINGS

To make this soup parve, do not add sausage. The mini matzo balls are a real treat and fun to eat.

MOZZARELLA, ARUGULA AND SUN-DRIED TOMATO SANDWICH

This sandwich sounds so fancy and tastes so good!

	Italian dressing	1	bunch arugula
1	French baguette, sliced in half lengthwise	1	cup chopped sun-dried tomatoes in oil
	Mozzarella cheese, plain, smoked or spiced		

Spread dressing on both sides of bread. Arrange mozzarella cheese on one side of bread. Layer arugula over cheese. Sprinkle with dressing. Spread tomatoes on other side of bread. Flip tomato side on top of cheese side. Stuff remaining arugula into sandwich. Press firmly to secure sandwich. Wrap tightly in foil. Let stand for 30 minutes. Remove foil and slice bread into 2 to 3-inch sandwiches.

YIELD: 4 TO 6 SERVINGS

SHALOM Y'ALL SANDWICH "THE KOSHER" BLT

½ pound beef fry, cubed
Guacamole
White sandwich bread, crusts
  trimmed and toasted

Lettuce leaves
Tomato, sliced

Heat skillet to medium high. Sauté beef until done. Spread guacamole on toast. Top with lettuce, tomato, and beef. Top with second piece of toast. Cut sandwiches in half on diagonal to make triangle sandwiches.

YIELD: 4 SERVINGS

May substitute pastrami or corned beef for beef fry.

GUACAMOLE

2 avocados, mashed

¼ teaspoon chili powder

1 tablespoon lemon juice

⅓ cup diced tomatoes

⅓ cup mayonnaise

Dash of cayenne pepper

1 tablespoon grated onion

1 teaspoon Kosher salt

Blend avocados, chili powder, lemon juice, tomatoes, mayonnaise, cayenne, onion, and salt until smooth.

FISH'WICHES

1 cup light mayonnaise

2¼ teaspoons lemon zest, divided

¾ cup lemon juice, divided

1 cup loosely packed basil leaves

2 pounds firm white fish, cooked

2 tablespoons olive oil

¼ teaspoon salt

¼ teaspoon pepper

4 French bread rolls, halved

4 romaine lettuce leaves

¼ cup thinly sliced red onion

Process mayonnaise, 2 teaspoons lemon zest, ¼ cup lemon juice, and basil in food processor until smooth, stopping to scrape down sides. Store in an airtight container in refrigerator for up to 1 week.

Flake fish in a medium bowl. Add ¼ teaspoon lemon zest, ¼ cup lemon juice, oil, salt, and pepper. Toss gently to coat. Spread basil mayonnaise evenly on cut side of rolls. Place lettuce and fish on bottom halves of rolls. Top with red onion and cover with top roll.

YIELD: 4 SERVINGS

STATE FAIR KOSHER FRIED DILLS

Yum, yum, yum, y'all!

½ cup all-purpose flour

¼ cup beer

3 dashes Tabasco sauce

1 tablespoon paprika

2 teaspoons garlic salt

1 teaspoon salt

1 tablespoon cayenne pepper or to taste

1 tablespoon pepper

Vegetable oil

5 dill pickles, sliced ⅛-inch thick

Hot or honey mustard for garnish

Combine flour, beer, Tabasco, paprika, garlic salt, salt, cayenne, and pepper. Mix well. Heat oil over medium-high heat in skillet. Dip pickle into batter. Fry 4 minutes or until pickle floats to surface. Drain well. Serve with hot or honey mustard.

GOAT CHEESE, CARROT AND GREEN OLIVE TAPENADE SANDWICHES

CARROTS

2	tablespoons sugar	¼	teaspoon cayenne pepper
1	tablespoon lemon juice	1	teaspoon salt
2	tablespoons sweet paprika	¼	cup olive oil
1	teaspoon ground cumin	1½	pounds julienne cut carrots (8 carrots)
½	teaspoon cinnamon		

CARROTS

Whisk together sugar, lemon juice, paprika, cumin, cinnamon, cayenne, salt, and oil until sugar dissolves. Cook carrots in a 4-5 quart pot in boiling salted water for 45 seconds until crisp-tender. Drain well in colander. Immediately toss with dressing. Cool to room temperature, stirring occasionally. Cover and refrigerate at least 4 hours.

TAPENADE

1¼	cups green olives, pitted	1	teaspoon finely grated lemon zest
3	tablespoons capers, drained and rinsed	1½	tablespoons lemon juice
¼	cup chopped flat leaf parsley	½	teaspoon pepper
		¼	cup olive oil

TAPENADE

Pulse olives, capers, parsley, zest, lemon juice, and pepper in a food processor until coarsely chopped. Scrape down sides and slowly add oil while pulsing until mixture is finely chopped but not a paste.

SANDWICHES

12	slices good quality pumpernickel sandwich bread	6 ounces soft mild goat cheese, softened

SANDWICHES

Spread olive tapenade on 6 bread slices. Spread goat cheese on remaining bread slices. Place carrot on top of tapenade and press goat cheese slice on top, pressing together. May wrap in foil at least 1 hour to seal sandwiches.

YIELD: 6 SERVINGS

The green olive tapenade may be used as a spread with toasted French bread slices.
The carrots may be served as a side dish. They are quite flavorful!

CRUNCHY CHICKEN SALAD SANDWICHES

DRESSING

½ cup mayonnaise

2 tablespoons Dijon mustard

1 teaspoon salt

½ teaspoon pepper

Whisk dressing ingredients and set aside.

SALAD

3 chicken breasts, bone in
   Salt and pepper to taste

2 ribs celery, diced

2 scallions, sliced

¼ cup finely chopped red onion

½ cup chopped red bell pepper

½ cup toasted almonds slivers

1 loaf white bread

Season the chicken with salt and pepper and roast on a foil lined baking sheet in 350 degree oven for about 45 minutes or until just cooked through. When cool enough to handle, discard skin and bones and chop chicken breast meat into bite-sized pieces.

Add celery, scallions, onion, bell pepper, and almonds to chicken pieces. Add dressing to chicken mixture. Spread on white bread or croissant to create sandwiches.

The flavors will "mingle" better if the dressing is mixed in while the chicken is still slightly warm. Refrigerate until ready to serve. You might want to add the sliced scallions, onions, pepper, and nuts on the day of serving so the nuts will remain crunchy and the onion flavor does not become too strong.

CITRUS SALTED SWEET POTATO CHIPS

Serve bowls of these instead of nuts. Have enough for refills—you will need them!

Zest of 1 lime

Zest of ½ orange

2-3 teaspoons kosher salt
   or to taste

3 large sweet potatoes

Vegetable oil

Combine lime zest, orange zest and salt. Shave strips of potatoes with vegetable peeler. Heat 1-2 inches oil in a skillet over medium-high heat. Fry potato strips in batches for 1-2 minutes. Transfer to paper towel-lined dish. Sprinkle with zest/salt mixture.

YIELD: 4 TO 6 SERVINGS

Salads

To my mother Diane Friedman

Some of my fondest childhood memories were at the family dinner table
enjoying your delicious Southern cooking. Your kindness shall never be forgotten.

Love,

Paul M. Friedman, MD

Tania Ades Blotner was raised in the Syrian community of Brooklyn, New York. From childhood, she was always exposed to the unique styles of Syrian cooking which blends Mediterranean, Lebanese, and various Sephardic influences. In 2001, Tania moved to New Orleans and, most recently, relocated to Memphis, in the wake of Hurricane Katrina. In Memphis, she has learned how to cook and entertain "Kosher Southern". However, moving from North to South meant changing more than just her cooking style. Tania has become proficient in serving true Southern-style buffet service. Although Northerners may plate food or, alternately, pass dishes around the table, Southerners serve every meal as a buffet, arranging the buffet tables into elegant expressions of visually engaging, edible artwork. Tania's unique blend of Syrian cuisine mixed with Southern classic cuisine served buffet-style proves that when you mix two cherished techniques, a new and wonderful tradition is created.

AMAZING AVOCADO CORN SALSA

2	tablespoons vegetable oil	½	cup chopped green onion
4	cups fresh or frozen corn kernels	¼	cup chopped fresh cilantro
1	tablespoon taco seasoning	¼	cup fresh lime juice
½	teaspoon pepper	2	tablespoons orange juice
1	sweet red bell pepper, chopped	1	teaspoon salt
½	jalapeño pepper, seeded and chopped	3	ripe avocados, diced

Heat oil in a skillet. Sauté corn, taco seasoning, and pepper 6-8 minutes or until corn is slightly golden browned. Combine corn mixture with red pepper, jalapeño pepper, green onion, cilantro, lime juice, orange juice, and salt. Mix well. Refrigerate for 30 minutes. Stir in avocados just before serving.

YIELD: 8 SERVINGS

To easily remove pit from avocado, slice completely around the pit and twist each half in opposite directions. Pull apart and remove the pit. If flesh is firm, tap the pit firmly with the knife and twist the blade to lift out. If the flesh is soft, gently squeeze the avocado and remove the pit with your fingers.

WALDORF SALAD

A time-tested classic enjoyed for generations but the twist is the pears and honey!

3	green and/or red apples, cored and chopped	1	cup raisins
2	pears, cored and chopped	1	cup chopped walnuts
2	stalks celery, chopped	1	cup mayonnaise
		1	tablespoon honey

Combine apple, pear, celery, raisins, and walnuts. Add enough mayonnaise and honey to coat mixture.

YIELD: 6 SERVINGS

JICAMA SALAD WITH LEMON VINAIGRETTE DRESSING

Also known as a Mexican potato or a Mexican turnip, jicama is the perfect partner for a cool, crisp salad. This is great in the summer when cilantro and peppers are in season!

LEMON VINAIGRETTE

7	tablespoons lemon juice	1	teaspoon sugar
2	tablespoons Dijon mustard	½	cup olive oil

LEMON VINAIGRETTE

Whisk together lemon juice, mustard, sugar, and oil until blended.

SALAD

2	jicama, peeled and julienne cut	2	orange peppers, cored and julienne cut
2	sweet red peppers, cored and julienne cut	¼	cup chopped cilantro
2	yellow peppers, cored and julienne cut		

SALAD

Combine jicama, all peppers, and cilantro in a bowl. Pour on ½ cup lemon vinaigrette and toss to coat.

YIELD: 6 TO 8 SERVINGS

Julienne is long, rectangular cuts, such as, a matchstick. Core the peppers and then slice them in thin strips. Cut a thin slice from one side of the jicama to stabilize it. Slice the jicama lengthwise making thin parallel cuts. Stack these slices and make a second set of cuts through the stack. Julienne should be very narrow ¼-inch thick.

BROCCOLI RAISIN SALAD

Tantalizing to both the eyes and the mouth.

DRESSING

1 cup mayonnaise	¼ cup white vinegar
½ cup sugar	

DRESSING

Whisk together mayonnaise, sugar, and vinegar until smooth.

SALAD

2-3 stalks broccoli or	1 cup sunflower seeds
2 packages florets	½ cup raisins
¼ cup finely chopped green onion	

SALAD

Combine broccoli florets, green onion, sunflower seeds, and raisins. Pour on dressing and toss to coat.

YIELD: 4 TO 6 SERVINGS

Best to let salad marinate for several hours or overnight.

Broccoli can be refrigerated unwashed in an air-tight bag for up to four days. It is an excellent source of Vitamins A and C. It is widely available fresh year round but the peak season is from October to April. Choose broccoli that is dark green with tight buds and firm, blemish-free stems.

PEACHES AND TOMATO SALAD

*These two unlikely fruits pair up for a taste that says summer! Best to
make this salad in the summer—August is when they are at their peak of ripeness!*

3	tablespoons olive oil	3	large red tomatoes, sliced and halved
1	tablespoon balsamic vinegar	1½	cups cherry tomatoes
1	tablespoon lemon juice	½	cup chopped celery
¾	teaspoon salt, divided		Pepper to taste
½	teaspoon pepper, divided	¼	cup chopped mint leaves
4	large peaches (1½ pounds), quartered		

Whisk together oil, vinegar, lemon juice, ½ teaspoon salt, and ¼ teaspoon pepper in a bowl. Set aside. Arrange peaches, tomatoes, cherry tomatoes, and celery on a serving platter. Sprinkle with ¼ teaspoon salt and pepper. Add mint to vinaigrette. Pour over salad.

YIELD: 8 TO 10 SERVINGS

Salads

LEMON BASIL CHICKEN SALAD

A perky salad bursting with fresh and sunny flavors!

DRESSING

1¾ cups mayonnaise

1 tablespoon lemon zest

3 tablespoons lemon juice

1 tablespoon white wine (optional)

¾ teaspoon kosher salt

⅛ teaspoon pepper

DRESSING

Whisk together mayonnaise, lemon zest, lemon juice, wine, salt, and pepper in a large bowl until smooth.

CHICKEN SALAD

2½ quarts water

5 pounds boneless skinless chicken breast halves

2 cups snow peas or 1 (8 ounce) package sugar snap peas

2 cups loosely packed basil, coarsely chopped

1 cup green or red seedless grapes, halved

CHICKEN SALAD

Bring water to boil. Add chicken. Cover, reduce heat and simmer until chicken is done and opaque in center. Drain and cool. Cut chicken into bite size pieces. Add to dressing and toss to coat. Add snow peas, basil and grapes. Toss to coat. Cover and refrigerate at least 1 hour.

YIELD: 12 SERVINGS

SIMPLE TOMATO DILL SALAD

We love our tomatoes in the South. All summer they grow
in abundance and you can always find some great way to eat them!
Some people just bite into them like an apple-that is just how good they are!
This is a light but satisfying refresher on a sultry summer day.

3 tablespoons vinegar

3 tablespoons sugar

2 teaspoons vegetable oil

4 tomatoes, sliced

1 red onion, sliced

1 tablespoon chopped fresh dill

Whisk together vinegar, sugar, and oil. Pour over tomatoes and red onion. Sprinkle with dill.

YIELD: 6 TO 8 SERVINGS

TOMATOES AND SWEET ONIONS

*Sweet onions and fresh summer tomatoes...this dressing
brings out the best in both...it gets better and better each day!*

DRESSING

⅓ cup balsamic vinegar
⅓ cup sugar
1 teaspoon salt

1 teaspoon soy sauce
1 cup vegetable oil

DRESSING

Whisk together vinegar, sugar, salt, and soy sauce. Slowly whisk in oil until blended.

SALAD

5-6 tomatoes, sliced
2 sweet onions, sliced
1 tablespoon dried parsley

1 teaspoon garlic powder
1 teaspoon dried oregano
1 teaspoon Italian seasoning

SALAD

Layer tomatoes and onion on a serving platter. Sprinkle with parsley, garlic powder, oregano, and seasoning. Pour dressing over tomato and onion. Refrigerate overnight.

YIELD: 8 TO 10 SERVINGS

MINT BEANS

1½ pounds green beans
¾ cup olive oil
½ cup chopped fresh mint
¼ cup red wine vinegar
¾ teaspoon salt

½ teaspoon minced garlic
¼ teaspoon fresh pepper
1 cup toasted walnuts, chopped
1 cup diced red onion
1 cup feta cheese

Cook beans in boiling water for 5 minutes. Plunge beans in ice cold water to stop cooking process. Blend oil, mint, vinegar, salt, garlic, and pepper in food processor until smooth. Pour dressing over beans and toss to coat. Top with walnuts, red onion, and feta cheese.

YIELD: 4 SERVINGS

This bean salad is also great without the feta cheese.

Salads

62

BEAN SALAD

DRESSING

2½ cups white vinegar

1 cup vegetable oil

2 cups sugar

3 tablespoons salt

Pepper to taste

DRESSING

Blend vinegar, oil, sugar, salt, and pepper until smooth.

SALAD

1 (15 ounce) can French cut green beans, drained

1 (15 ounce) can peas, drained

1 (8 ounce) can water chestnuts, drained

1 (4 ounce) jar whole mushrooms, drained

1 (15 ounce) can mini yellow corn, drained

1 (2 ounce) jar pimentos, drained

1 onion, thinly sliced

1 cup diced celery

1 cauliflower, cut into florets

1 cup sliced carrots

SALAD

Combine green beans, peas, water chestnuts, mushrooms, corn, pimentos, onion, celery, cauliflower, and carrot in a large bowl. Pour on dressing and toss to coat.

YIELD: 10 TO 12 SERVINGS

This bean salad will keep in the refrigerator for two weeks.

TOMATO AND WATERMELON MEDLEY

Two Southern summer staples met, married and make beautiful music together.

5 cups cubed seeded watermelon

1½ pounds ripe tomatoes, cut into ¾-inch cubes

3 teaspoons sugar

½ teaspoon salt

1 small red onion, quartered and thinly sliced

⅓ cup red wine vinegar

⅓ cup olive oil

Lettuce leaves

Pepper to taste

Combine watermelon and tomatoes in a large bowl. Sprinkle with sugar and salt. Let stand for 10 minutes. Stir in red onion, vinegar, and oil. Cover and refrigerate for 2 hours. Serve on a bed of lettuce leaves. Sprinkle with pepper.

YIELD: 6 TO 8 SERVINGS

Salads

GONE FISHIN'...DIXIE CAVIAR

*Who needs fish eggs y'all? Black-eyed peas are the pearls
of the South! This salad is quick, economical, easy, healthy, yummy,
and memorable! Perfect for a New Year's Day football fest!*

4 cups canned black-eyed peas	4 green onions, chopped
1 cup julienne cut yellow pepper	1-2 jalapeño peppers, seeded and chopped
1 cup Italian salad dressing	1-2 garlic cloves, minced
1 cup chopped tomatoes	⅓ cup chopped flat leaf parsley
¼ cup chopped red onion	

Combine black-eyed peas, pepper, dressing, tomatoes, red onion, green onion, jalapeño pepper, garlic, and parsley. Toss to coat.

YIELD: 6 TO 8 SERVINGS

Spoon salad on a bed of lettuce to serve. It is colorful and tasty!

NEW RED POTATOES AND GREEN BEAN SALAD

½ pound green beans, trimmed	½ cup basil leaves (12)
1½ pounds new red potatoes	1 garlic clove, minced
½ red onion, thinly sliced	⅓ cup extra virgin olive oil
1 cup chopped flat leaf parsley, divided	Salt and pepper to taste
Zest of 1 lemon	2 plum tomatoes, seeded and thinly sliced lengthwise
Juice of 1 lemon	

Cook beans in salted boiling water, covered, for 2 minutes. Drain and plunge into ice cold water. Cook potatoes in a separate pot of boiling water until tender. Drain and cool. Quarter potatoes. Combine green beans, potatoes, red onion, and ½ cup parsley in a shallow bowl. Blend lemon zest, lemon juice, ½ cup parsley, basil, and garlic in a food processor. Slowly add oil until smooth. Add salt and pepper. Pour dressing over green bean/potato mixture. Top with tomatoes. Refrigerate for 2 hours or overnight.

YIELD: 6 TO 8 SERVINGS

EGG AND OLIVE POTATO SALAD

A contemporary fusion of two classic Southern favorites! Small, red, waxy potatoes hold their shape when sliced or diced and do not absorb excessive dressing or become mushy.

3	pounds red potatoes	1	large stalk celery, diced
1	teaspoon salt	½	small sweet onion, grated
5	hard-boiled eggs, grated	1½	cups mayonnaise
1	(7 ounce) jar pimento-stuffed olives, drained and chopped	½	teaspoon pepper
			Paprika to taste

Cook potatoes in salted boiling water until tender. Drain and cool. Peel potatoes if preferred and cut into 1-inch cubes. Combine eggs, olive, celery, onion, mayonnaise, and pepper in a large bowl. Add potatoes and toss gently to coat. Cover and refrigerate for 2 hours. Sprinkle with paprika.

YIELD: 8 SERVINGS

Salads

PURDY POTATO SALAD

This recipe is a European Style potato salad and is very delicious.
It made a big hit at one of our tasting parties.

3	pounds medium Yukon gold potatoes	1	tablespoon reserved caper liquid
½	cup finely chopped chives	1	teaspoon coarse grain Dijon mustard
½	cup chopped parsley	½	cup extra virgin olive oil
2	tablespoons capers, drained and reserving liquid		Salt and pepper to taste
3	tablespoons white vinegar		

Cook potatoes in large pot of salted boiling water 20-30 minutes until tender. Drain and cool. Cut potatoes into ⅓-inch slices. Place in a large serving dish. Whisk together chives, parsley, capers, vinegar, caper liquid, mustard, and oil. Add salt and pepper. Pour dressing over potatoes and toss gently. Let stand at room temperature up to 2 hours before serving.

YIELD: 8 TO 10 SERVINGS

Peel potatoes if desired before slicing.

MEMPHIS' FAVORITE COLESLAW

This is a classic coleslaw recipe that is mayonnaise based.

DRESSING

1½	cups real mayonnaise	1	tablespoon salt
¾	cup vinegar	¾	teaspoon pepper
¾	cup sugar		

DRESSING

Blend mayonnaise, vinegar, sugar, salt, and pepper with an electric mixer. Store in refrigerator.

COLESLAW

1	large head green cabbage, chopped	1	large bell pepper, sliced

COLESLAW

Combine cabbage and pepper in a large bowl. Pour on dressing and toss to coat. Refrigerate.

YIELD: 6 TO 8 SERVINGS

CRUNCHY COLESLAW

This is one of those slaws you cannot stop eating! Crunchy, crunchy, crunchy!

DRESSING
⅓ cup vegetable oil

¼ cup rice or tarragon vinegar

2 tablespoons sugar

DRESSING
Whisk together oil, vinegar and sugar until sugar dissolves.

SALAD
1 package coleslaw mixture with carrots

3-4 green onions, sliced

1 cup frozen peas, thawed

1 package chicken flavored Ramen noodle soup, crushed

2 tablespoons toasted sesame seeds

3-4 ounces toasted slivered almonds

SALAD
Combine coleslaw, green onion, and peas. Stir in crushed noodles, sesame seeds, and almond. Pour on dressing 30 minutes before serving. Gently toss to coat to maintain crunchiness.

YIELD: 6 SERVINGS

Prepare salad and dressing on Friday and store separately. Toss together on Saturday for a delicious addition to a Sabbath lunch menu.

CRAB COLESLAW

In the South, we take our slaw seriously. There are many combinations of this versatile cold salad that usually start with shredded cabbage.

1 package imitation crab, chopped

1 (10 ounce) package coleslaw

1 pint cherry tomatoes, halved

1 (4 ounce) can black olives, sliced

1 tablespoon capers

3 tablespoons chopped basil

3 tablespoons chopped chives

1 cup mayonnaise

Salt and pepper to taste

Combine crab, coleslaw, tomatoes, olives, capers, basil, chives, mayonnaise, salt, and pepper. Mix well. Refrigerate before serving.

YIELD: 6 SERVINGS

CELERY ROOT SLAW

This slaw is a hit with everyone! This rather ugly, knobby brown vegetable is also known as celeriac and cultivated for its root. The flavor and texture is a cross between celery, parsley and potato. It is great in salads, stews, soups, or roasted with vegetables.

½ **seedless cucumber, coarsely grated or julienne cut**
1 **pound celery root, peeled, coarsely grated or julienne cut**
1 **cup mayonnaise**
½ **cup capers, drained and rinsed**

½ **cup chopped basil**
1 **teaspoon minced garlic**
1 **tablespoon lemon juice**
¼ **teaspoon salt**
¼ **teaspoon pepper**

Place cucumber in a sieve and press to discard excess liquid. Transfer to a bowl. Add celery root, mayonnaise, capers, basil, garlic, lemon juice, salt, and pepper. Mix well. Cover and refrigerate at least 1 hour or overnight.

YIELD: 4 TO 6 SERVINGS

Choose small, firm celery root that is heavy for its size. Avoid those with soft spots. Keep it refrigerated in a plastic bag for up to a week. It is necessary to cut off the knob-like protrusions or rootlets and the peel before slicing or dicing, or, in the case of the slaw, shredding the celery root for usage. You can keep the shredded celery root in an airtight plastic bag overnight and put the slaw together the next day.

ASIAN CUCUMBER SALAD

Yum, sweet and tangy.

2   large cucumbers, thinly sliced (seedless), peeled (optional)

2   teaspoons salt

2   tablespoons low sodium soy sauce

2   tablespoons sugar or artificial sweetener to taste

½   cup rice vinegar

Combine cucumber, salt, soy sauce, sugar, and vinegar. Mix well. Refrigerate at least 2 hours before serving. Garnish with fresh dill!

YIELD: 4 SERVINGS

Whole cucumbers can be stored unwashed in a plastic bag in the refrigerator for up to ten days. Cut cucumbers can be refrigerated, tightly wrapped for up to five days.

Pair the Asian Cucumber Salad with the Quickie Thai Curry and some white rice for a contrasting flavorful meal!

SOUTHWESTERN PASTA SALAD

Classic Tex-Mex ingredients like cilantro, lime juice and jalapeño peppers add kicky fiesta to the pasta. Olé!

¼-½   cup corn oil

⅓   cup lime juice

⅓   cup chopped cilantro

3   jalapeño peppers, diced

2   garlic cloves, minced

¾   teaspoon ground cumin

¾   teaspoon salt

1   avocado, chopped

8   ounces small pasta, cooked al dente

1   cup canned black beans

¾   cup chopped red onion

1   sweet red pepper, diced

1   yellow pepper, diced

Whisk together oil, lime juice, cilantro, jalapeño, garlic, cumin, and salt. Add avocado, pasta, black beans, red onion, red pepper, and yellow pepper. Mix well until coated in dressing.

YIELD: 4 SERVINGS

CHICKEN, CABBAGE AND NOODLES IN PEANUT SAUCE

A cool salad heated with Serrano chiles. Serve extra
peanut sauce on the side. Great to use leftover chicken!

PEANUT SAUCE

2 tablespoons minced ginger	⅔ cup lime juice
2 shallots, chopped	1 cup creamy peanut butter
¼ cup chicken broth	¼ cup sesame seed oil
⅓ cup soy sauce	

PEANUT SAUCE

Whisk together ginger, shallots, broth, soy sauce, lime juice, peanut butter, and oil until smooth. May refrigerate for 4-5 days.

SALAD

3-5 pounds cooked boneless, skinless chicken breast halves	2 jalapeño pepper, seeded, ribs removed and chopped
1 pound vermicelli pasta	½ cup loosely packed mint leaves, chopped
½ head green cabbage, shredded	½ cup roasted unsalted peanuts
1 cup shredded carrots	

SALAD

Combine chicken, pasta, cabbage, carrot, jalapeño pepper, mint, 1 cup peanut sauce, and peanuts. Toss until well mixed.

YIELD: 6 TO 8 SERVINGS

CHICKEN FOR DIPPING ON A STICK WITH PEANUT SAUCE

Soak bamboo skewers in water for 15 minutes.
Pound 2 pounds of chicken breasts and cut into strips.
Thread strips onto skewers and season with salt and pepper
(can add chili powder, cumin or curry powder). Grill the skewers for
1-2 minutes on each side until chicken is cooked. Arrange skewers
on a platter with the peanut sauce for dipping. You can
use beef threaded on the sticks as well.

ORZO SALAD WITH ROASTED CARROTS AND DILL

The combination of roasted carrots and orzo
makes this dish hearty and satisfying, but not heavy.

3 pounds carrots	Juice of 2 lemons
4 garlic cloves, unpeeled	4 green onions, white and light
¼ cup extra virgin olive oil, divided	green part, coarsely chopped
Coarse salt	½ cup loosely packed dill, chopped
1 pound orzo	Pepper to taste
Zest of 2 lemons	

Preheat oven to 450 degrees. Cut carrots diagonally into 2-inch pieces. Place on a rimmed baking sheet with garlic. Drizzle with 2 tablespoons oil and pinch of salt. Toss to coat. Roast at 450 degrees 15 minutes or until tender and browned. Cool. Squeeze garlic from skin. Mince to form a coarse paste.

Cook orzo in salted boiling water 7 minutes until al dente. Drain and immediately toss with 2 tablespoons oil. Cool. Add roasted carrots.

In a small bowl, combine lemon zest, lemon juice, green onion, and garlic paste. Stir in dill and pour over orzo mixture. Mix well. Sprinkle with salt and pepper. Serve or store covered with plastic wrap in refrigerator up to 1 day. Bring to room temperature before serving.

YIELD: 8 TO 10 SERVINGS

May prepare recipe in steps in advance.

DON'T FORGET TO EAT YOUR PEAS AND CARROTS

Steam two pounds of snap peas about 5 minutes
and then immerse in cold water. Roast carrots as above.
Combine carrots and snap peas. Add salt and pepper to taste.
Serve with warm brown rice and the Steak-like Shoulder Roast.

ORZO SALAD WITH DRIED CRANBERRIES AND CARAMELIZED ALMONDS

CARAMELIZED ALMONDS
1 cup chopped almonds

¾ cup sugar

CARAMELIZED ALMONDS

Spray a skillet with oil. Add almonds and sugar. Cook and stir constantly over low heat until almonds are golden browned and caramelized.

SALAD
1 package orzo, cooked al dente
½ cup vegetable oil
¼ cup vinegar
2 teaspoons sugar

2 teaspoons honey mustard
Garlic powder and pepper to taste
½ cup dried cranberries

SALAD

Place orzo in a bowl. In a separate bowl, whisk together oil, vinegar, sugar, mustard, garlic powder, and pepper. Pour dressing over orzo. Stir in cranberries. Top with caramelized almonds.

YIELD: 6 TO 8 SERVINGS

RICE AND ARTICHOKE SALAD

A favorite side dish salad with savory meat or chicken dishes!
This salad can seem elegant or down-home!

2 (6 ounce) boxes chicken flavored rice mix
¼ cup chopped roasted red peppers
16 pimento-stuffed green olives, sliced
½ cup chopped green onion

2 (14 ounce) cans artichoke hearts, drained and chopped
½ cup mayonnaise
½ cup Italian salad dressing
1 teaspoon curry powder

Cook rice according to package directions. Transfer to a bowl to cool. Add red pepper, olive, and green onion. Add artichokes. In a separate bowl, blend mayonnaise, Italian dressing, and curry. Pour dressing over rice mixture and toss to coat. Refrigerate until ready to serve.

YIELD: 8 SERVINGS

SIMPLE SOUTHWEST-FLAVORED QUINOA SALAD

*With its light fluffy texture, quinoa is a great alternative to
white rice or couscous. It is also kosher to use on Passover.*

1   (16 ounce) can corn niblets,
    drained, reserving liquid
1   cup quinoa
1   (16 ounce) can black beans,
    drained and rinsed
1   red onion, sliced
3   tablespoons chopped cilantro

1   avocado, diced
½   teaspoon garlic salt
    Pepper to taste
2   tablespoons lemon juice
2   tablespoons olive oil

Pour reserved corn liquid in a 2 cup measuring cup. Add enough water to equal 2 cups and pour into a saucepan. Bring to boil. Add quinoa and cook for 15 minutes. Remove from heat and let stand for 5 minutes. Gently stir in corn, black beans, red onion, cilantro, avocado, garlic salt, pepper, lemon juice, and oil. Refrigerate.

YIELD: 4 SERVINGS

RICE SALAD WITH SUGAR SNAP PEAS, MINT AND LIME

2   cups water
1   teaspoon salt
1⅓ cups rice
2   cups sugar snap peas
½   cup chopped mint
½   cup chopped green onions

3   tablespoons olive oil
2   tablespoons fresh lime juice
2   tablespoons peeled and julienne
    cut ginger
1   teaspoon sugar
    Salt and pepper to taste

Bring water and salt to boil. Add rice. Reduce heat, cover and cook for 15 minutes. Let stand for 5 minutes. Cool completely in a large bowl. Cook sugar snap peas in salted boiling water for 1 minute. Drain and rinse under cold water. Drain well. Add to rice. Stir in mint, green onion, oil, lime juice, ginger, sugar, salt, and pepper.

YIELD: 4 TO 6 SERVINGS

This recipe can also be made by substituting asparagus, zucchini, or baby peas for the sugar snap peas.

COUSCOUS WITH CHICKPEAS, TOMATOES AND EDAMAME

A protein packed dish that blends the best of North Africa,
India and the Deep South! It makes a great meatless main dish.

1 tablespoon olive oil	1 cup halved grape tomatoes
1 cup frozen shelled edamame	2 cups parve chicken soup base
½ teaspoon crushed red pepper	¼ teaspoon salt
2 teaspoons minced garlic	1 cup couscous, uncooked
¼ cup water	1½ cups chopped green onions
¼ cup chopped fresh basil	1 cup chopped feta cheese
1 (16 ounce) can chickpeas, drained and rinsed	

Heat oil in a large skillet over medium heat. Add edamame, red pepper, and garlic. Cook, stirring frequently, for 3 minutes. Add water, basil, chickpeas, and tomatoes. Simmer for 15 minute. Add chicken base and salt. Bring to boil. Gradually stir in couscous. Remove from heat and cover. Let stand for 5 minutes. Stir in green onion and feta cheese. Serve warm or chilled.

YIELD: 6 SERVINGS

OLD-FASHIONED LAYERED SALAD

Serve in a trifle dish for an elegant, mouth-watering presentation.

2 cups mayonnaise	1 (8 ounce) package shredded Cheddar cheese
1 tablespoon milk	1 (10 ounce) package frozen peas, thawed
1 teaspoon dry mustard	1 medium red onion, diced
½ teaspoon salt	6 hard-boiled eggs, chopped
½ teaspoon pepper	1½ cups imitation bacon
1 head romaine or iceberg lettuce, coarsely chopped	1 large cucumber, seeded and chopped

Whisk together mayonnaise, milk, mustard, salt, and pepper. Layer half of each, lettuce, Cheddar cheese, peas, red onion, eggs, bacon, and cucumber in a serving bowl. Spread half dressing over top. Repeat all layers. Top with remaining dressing. Cover and refrigerate for several hours.

YIELD: 6 TO 8 SERVINGS

Salads

SUPERFOODS SALAD

1 cup spinach, torn into bite-size pieces	¼ cup chickpeas, rinsed and drained
1 cup chopped romaine lettuce	½ cup grated carrot
¼ cup shredded red cabbage	1 avocado, cubed
½ cup sliced sweet red pepper	2 tablespoons olive oil
½ tomato, chopped	1 teaspoon balsamic vinegar

Combine spinach, romaine, cabbage, pepper, tomato, chickpeas, carrot, and avocado. In a separate bowl, whisk together oil and vinegar. Just before serving, pour on dressing. Toss to coat.

YIELD: 4 SERVINGS

Buy all ingredients and make separate salads for lunch on-the-go all week! Packed with fiber, iron, vitamins, antioxidants and flavor!

May add Monterey Jack cheese, hard-boiled eggs or turkey for protein.

PARMESAN ALMOND SALAD TOPPERS

½ cup finely shredded or grated Parmesan cheese　　¼ cup sliced almonds

Preheat oven to 400 degrees. Combine Parmesan cheese and almonds. Drop mixture in 8 mounds on a greased or parchment paper-lined baking sheet. Flatten each pile. Bake at 400 degrees for 6-7 minutes or until crisp. Cool for 10 minutes. Store in an airtight container for up to 3 days.

HODGE PODGE SALAD

This salad is a winner. It is great with or without bleu cheese.
It is perfect as a starter for a casual dinner or as a one-dish meal for lunch!

DRESSING
½ teaspoon salt
½ teaspoon pepper
½ teaspoon dried parsley

2 tablespoons white wine vinegar
¼ cup vegetable oil
2 tablespoons sugar

DRESSING

Whisk together salt, pepper, parsley, vinegar, oil, and sugar until well blended.

SALAD
1 head romaine lettuce, chopped or 1 package
1 (11 ounce) can Mandarin oranges, drained
1 avocado, chopped
1 green apple, chopped

4 green onions, chopped
¼ cup dried cranberries
½ cup slivered almonds, toasted
½ cup bleu cheese, crumbled (optional)
1 tablespoon sugar

SALAD

Combine lettuce, oranges, avocado, apple, green onion, cranberries, almonds, bleu cheese, and sugar in a bowl. Pour on dressing and toss to coat.

YIELD: 4 SERVINGS

MAMA'S MUSHROOM ROLL-UPS

Make plenty of these because your family will eat them as they come out of the oven!

1 (16 ounce) package mushrooms, chopped
1 onion, finely chopped
4-5 tablespoons margarine
1 tablespoon all-purpose flour

Salt and pepper to taste
⅓ cup water
1 loaf white sandwich bread
Margarine, melted

Preheat broiler. Sauté mushrooms and onion in margarine. Sprinkle with flour, salt and pepper. Slowly stir in water. Remove bread crusts and roll bread thin. Spread mushroom mixture over bread and roll up. Dip rolls into melted margarine and place on baking sheet. Broil both sides until golden browned. May freeze rolls before broiling.

Serve with any salad

Salads

WARM SALMON SALAD

2	tablespoons olive oil	½	cup golden raisins
½	pound salmon, cut into bite size pieces	¼	cup pine nut or craisins
½	sweet red pepper or ½ bell pepper, chopped	½	teaspoon salt
		1	(10 ounce) package baby spinach
½	yellow pepper, chopped		Balsamic vinegar

Combine oil, salmon, bell pepper, yellow pepper, raisins, nuts or craisins, and salt in a skillet. Sauté about 8 minutes until salmon is cooked. Spoon mixture over a bed of baby spinach. Drizzle with vinegar.

YIELD: 4 SERVINGS

Serving this salad with the warm salmon gives depth to the flavors. It can be served as an appetizer, for a luncheon or as a perfect weeknight meal.

LADIES LUNCHEON SALAD

These exact ingredients in these exact amounts come together in a perfect salad that everyone will request over and over!

1	cup sliced almonds	1	(11 ounce) can Mandarin oranges, drained
1	cup sugar	1	cup dried cranberries
3	packages Italian butter lettuce	½	cup olive oil
2	stalks celery, chopped	3	tablespoons wine vinegar
1	yellow pepper, chopped		Salt and pepper to taste

Combine almonds and sugar in a skillet over medium heat. Cook until almonds are sugar coated. Place on foil to cool then break up. Mix lettuce, celery and pepper in a bowl. Add Mandarin oranges, almonds and cranberries. Blend oil, vinegar, salt, and pepper. Pour dressing over salad and toss to coat.

YIELD: 8 TO 10 SERVINGS

CURRIED LAYERED SALAD

This can be a one-dish meal for a luncheon!

DRESSING
1   (8 ounce) jar mayonnaise

5   teaspoons curry powder

DRESSING
Blend mayonnaise and curry until smooth.

SALAD
    Mixed greens
1   large onion, sliced
1   large bell pepper, chopped
1   stalk celery, chopped
2   mushrooms, sliced
2   (8 ounce) cans small green peas

3   tablespoons sugar
1   (8 ounce) package shredded Cheddar cheese
    Parmesan cheese
    Imitation bacon-flavored pieces (optional)

SALAD
Layer ingredients in the following order in a serving bowl, mixed greens, onion, half dressing, pepper, celery, mushroom, peas, remaining dressing, sugar, Cheddar cheese, and Parmesan cheese. Cover with plastic wrap and refrigerate overnight. Top with bacon bits just before serving.

YIELD: 6 TO 8 SERVINGS

SPINACH, ARUGULA, BELGIAN ENDIVE SALAD TOPPED WITH WARM GOAT CHEESE

An easy to make salad that "sounds" fancy and complicated! Dazzle your guests!

1	large bunch spinach	8	ounces goat cheese
1	package arugula	1	cup chopped pecans
2	heads Belgian endive, rinsed and sliced	¾	cup olive oil
		¼	cup vinegar

Combine spinach, arugula, and endive in a bowl. Roll goat cheese into 1 to 2-inch balls. Roll balls in pecans. Place on greased baking sheet and flatten each ball. Broil cheese until browned.

Pour oil and vinegar over greens and toss to coat. Divide greens among plates. Place goat cheese disks over each salad.

YIELD: 8 TO 10 SERVINGS

FRUITY CHICKEN SALAD

The sweet juices of strawberries and kiwi unwittingly create a perky ally for the tangy dressing.

¾	cup sugar	3	cups chopped cooked chicken
⅓	cup red wine vinegar	6	cups torn fresh spinach
1	teaspoon salt	1	quart strawberries, sliced
1	teaspoon dry mustard	3	kiwi fruit, peeled and sliced
1	teaspoon minced fresh onion	1	cup sliced almonds, toasted (optional)
1	cup vegetable oil		
1	tablespoon poppy seeds (optional)		

Process sugar, vinegar, salt, mustard, and onion in blender until smooth. Turn on high speed and slowly add oil. Pour mixture into a serving bowl. Stir in poppy seeds. Add chicken and toss to coat. Refrigerate until ready to serve.

Arrange a bed of spinach on a serving platter. Mix strawberries and kiwi into chicken mixture. Spoon over spinach and top with almonds.

YIELD: 8 TO 10 SERVINGS

MOLASSES MARINATED MEAT SALAD WITH POPPY SEED DRESSING

MEAT AND MARINADE

½ cup molasses

¼ cup coarse grain mustard

1-2 pound skirt steak

MEAT AND MARINADE

Blend molasses and mustard. Pour over steak. Marinate for 2 hours or overnight. Grill or broil to desired degree of doneness. Cut steak into thin slices.

DRESSING

1 cup vegetable oil

¾ cup sugar

1 teaspoon dry mustard

2 tablespoons chopped onion

⅓ cup apple cider vinegar

1 teaspoon salt

1 tablespoon poppy seeds

DRESSING

Whisk together oil, sugar, mustard, onion, vinegar, salt, and poppy seeds until smooth.

SALAD

1-2 packages Bibb, romaine or iceberg lettuce

1 cucumber, diced

1 cup cubed mangoes

1 red onion, chopped

½ cup dried cranberries (optional)

SALAD

Arrange lettuce, cucumber, mango, red onion, and cranberries on platter. Place meat slices over salad. Drizzle dressing over all. Garnish with sliced apples.

YIELD: 4 SERVINGS

SALAMI, BARLEY AND PINE NUT SALAD

A hearty winter salad.

2	cups chicken broth	½	pound salami, cut into small chunks
1	cup quick-cooking barley, uncooked	3	tablespoons lemon juice
¾	chopped jarred roasted sweet red peppers	2	tablespoons extra virgin olive oil
1	small cucumber, diced	¾	teaspoon sugar
1	tablespoon chopped fresh dill	½	teaspoon salt
1	tablespoon chopped fresh parsley	½	teaspoon pepper
		2	tablespoons pine nuts, toasted

Bring chicken broth to boil. Stir in barley. Cover, reduce heat and simmer 10 minutes until tender. Remove from heat. Let stand covered for 5 minutes. Drain excess water.

Combine barley, pepper, cucumber, dill, parsley, and salami. Whisk together lemon juice, oil, sugar, salt, and pepper. Pour dressing over barley salad. Top with pine nuts.

YIELD: 6 SERVINGS

NIÇOISE SALAD DRESSING

*This salad dressing typifies the cuisine of Nice, a city on the French Riviera.
Their style is hot and cold ingredients in one dish. A salad with this dressing is a great
satisfying meal depending on the ingredients. A Niçoise salad should be served on a platter
with salad greens and any or all of the following ingredients: tomatoes, black olives, garlic,
anchovies, green beans, potatoes, tuna, onions, hard-cooked eggs, or cubed deli-meat.
Pour the dressing generously over the platter and serve.*

1	cup vegetable oil	2	teaspoons salt
¼	cup wine vinegar		Pepper to taste
2	teaspoons sugar	2-3	garlic cloves, minced
1	teaspoon dry mustard	2	tablespoons soy sauce
½	teaspoon paprika		

Combine oil, vinegar, sugar, mustard, paprika, salt, pepper, garlic, and soy sauce in a jar. Shake well until blended. Store in refrigerator.

YIELD: 4 TO 6 SERVINGS

LAYERED ANTIPASTO SALAD

Everyone loves the combination of this salad! It looks inviting and tastes divine!

NON-DAIRY CAESAR DRESSING

2-3	garlic cloves, minced	1	teaspoon dry mustard
2	eggs	½	teaspoon pepper
¾	cup olive oil	1	teaspoon salt
¼	cup vinegar		

NON-DAIRY CAESAR DRESSING

Combine garlic, eggs, oil, vinegar, mustard, pepper, and salt in a food processor. Process 5-10 minutes until creamy.

SALAD

3	cups penne pasta, uncooked	1	pound salami, chopped
2½	cups broccoli florets	1	cup black olives
1	tablespoon chopped parsley	1	onion, sliced and caramelized
2	cups chopped tomatoes		

SALAD

Cook pasta according to package direction. Add broccoli during last 2 minutes of cooking. Drain, rinse and cool. Toss with parsley. Spoon half pasta mixture into a glass bowl. Top with half each of tomatoes, salami, black olives, and onion. Repeat layers. Pour dressing evenly over salad. Cover and refrigerate at least 2 hours or overnight.

YIELD: 6 TO 8 SERVINGS

PARMESAN PEPPERCORN DRESSING

1½	cups vegetable oil	3	teaspoons chili sauce
½	cup white vinegar	1	teaspoon mustard
	Juice of 1½ lemons	¼	cup grated Parmesan cheese
½	teaspoon Worcestershire sauce		Salt and pepper to taste

Combine oil, vinegar, lemon juice, Worcestershire sauce, chili sauce, mustard, Parmesan cheese, salt, and pepper in a blender or food processor. Blend until smooth. Cover and refrigerate at least 1 hour.

YIELD: 2 CUPS

CAESAR SALAD DRESSING

The Challah croutons are the perfect match for this classic!

1½ cups vegetable oil
2 garlic cloves, minced
¼ cup lemon juice
1 egg
½ cup grated Parmesan cheese

1 tablespoon Worcestershire sauce
1 teaspoon pepper
½ teaspoon salt

Combine oil and garlic. Let stand for 1 hour. Drain oil and discard garlic. Blend oil, lemon juice, egg, Parmesan cheese, Worcestershire sauce, pepper, and salt.

YIELD: 8 SERVINGS

CHALLAY'ALL CHALLAH CROUTONS

Challah bread

3 tablespoons butter or margarine

3 tablespoons olive oil

2 tablespoons chopped tarragon

1 teaspoon salt

½ teaspoon pepper

Dash of garlic powder

2 teaspoons dried parsley

Freeze a loaf Challah bread. Cut into 1 to 2-inch cubes and arrange on a baking sheet. Bake at 200 degrees overnight.

Heat butter or margarine and oil in a large skillet. Stir in bread cubes until coated. Add tarragon, salt, pepper, garlic powder, and parsley. Cook and stir until croutons are coated and browned. Dry on baking sheet. Store in zip-top plastic bags. May also freeze.

YIELD: 8 SERVINGS

BLEU CHEESE DRESSING

¾ cup half & half
3 cups mayonnaise
1 cup sour cream
6-8 ounces bleu cheese
2 teaspoons garlic salt

Whisk together half & half, mayonnaise, sour cream, bleu cheese, and garlic salt until blended.

YIELD: 12 SERVINGS

MAYFAIR DRESSING

Don't tell anyone about the anchovies! They will never know but keep wondering what the intriguing flavor is in this dressing.

1 garlic clove, peeled
1 stalk celery, chopped
½ medium onion
1 (2 ounce) can flat anchovies
3 eggs
1 teaspoon pepper

½ teaspoon salt
½ teaspoon sugar
2 teaspoons mustard
1 tablespoon lemon juice
2 cups vegetable oil

Combine garlic, celery, onion, anchovies, eggs, pepper, salt, sugar, mustard, and lemon juice in a blender. Pulse for 1 minute. Add oil in a steady stream until smooth. Store in refrigerator for 2 weeks.

YIELD: 3 CUPS

Brunch & Dairy

In honor of our Mother, Bernice Cooper, with much love from

Laurie Cooper and Donald Emerson   ■   Debbi Cooper   ■   Cindy and Bart Ehrenkranz

Aileen and Pace Cooper   ■   Tova and David Cooper

Bernice Schramm fell in love with Irby Cooper while they both attended Washington University in St. Louis, Missouri. She quickly realized she would need to relocate to Memphis, where Irby was establishing his successful career. Her mother worried that her daughter would starve, fearing there were not enough Jews in Memphis to warrant accessible kosher foods. Bernice's friends in New York laughed when they heard she would soon be buying her kosher food from the local Piggly Wiggly grocery store.

Bernice arrived with an iron skillet in her hand and a determination to master the art of Southern cooking. She quickly developed a taste for cornbread, made in her iron skillet, cooking Southern delicacies like a true native daughter. She also began a sixty plus year commitment to community activism. "We wanted to open our doors to organizations outside of the Jewish community, while adhering to our religious standards. In this way, the kosher, observant Jews could participate in local political dinners and support the arts." Bernice, with her heated skillet and even warmer heart, has certainly made an impression on Memphis. As for her scoffing friends, they stopped laughing when they tasted her delectable kosher food, fresh from Piggly Wiggly.

HASH BROWNS CASSEROLE

1   (32 ounce) package frozen
    Southern style hash browns,
    thawed
1   stick butter, melted
1   (12 ounce) package shredded
    Cheddar cheese

1   (10¾ ounce) can cream of celery
    soup
1   (8 ounce) container sour cream
½   cup minced fresh onion
    Bread crumbs

Preheat oven to 350 degrees. Place hash browns in a greased 13 x 9 x 2-inch baking dish. Combine butter, Cheddar cheese, soup, sour cream, and onion. Pour mixture over hash browns. Cover and bake at 350 degrees for 1 hour, 5 minutes or until browned and bubbly. Uncover and sprinkle with bread crumbs. Bake an additional 10 minutes.

YIELD: 10 TO 12 SERVINGS

CLASSIC SOUTHERN PANCAKES

1   cup all-purpose flour
1   tablespoon sugar
2   teaspoons baking powder
¼   teaspoon salt

1   egg, beaten
1   cup milk
2   tablespoons vegetable oil

Combine flour, sugar, baking powder, and salt. In a separate bowl, blend egg, milk, and oil. Stir into flour mixture until blended but slightly lumpy. Heat a heavy greased skillet over medium heat. Pour ¼ cup batter into skillet. Cook and flip when pancake is bubbly and edges are dry. Cook until golden browned. Reduce heat and cook remaining batter.

YIELD: 4 SERVINGS

Looking for an alternative to syrup? Top pancakes with toasted pecans, sliced bananas or blueberries, and sprinkle with powdered sugar, cinnamon and nutmeg. We like the pancakes plain, but the toppings should be over the top!

COME AND GET IT BREAKFAST CASSEROLE

*Orange wedges would make a beautiful
accompaniment to this Sunday morning special!*

1 pound vegetable crumble (meat substitute)	1 (8 ounce) package shredded sharp Cheddar cheese
1 teaspoon ground fennel	6 large eggs
½ teaspoon ground sage	2 cups milk
½ teaspoon salt	1 teaspoon salt
¼ teaspoon pepper	1 teaspoon dry mustard
10 slices sandwich bread, cubed	¼ teaspoon Worcestershire sauce

Cook vegetable crumble with fennel, sage, salt, and pepper in a skillet until heated. Place bread cubes on a lightly greased 13 x 9 x 2-inch baking dish. Sprinkle evenly with Cheddar cheese. Top evenly with vegetable crumble mixture. Whisk together eggs, milk, salt, mustard, and Worcestershire sauce. Pour egg mixture over all. Cover and refrigerate for 8 hours or overnight.

Let stand at room temperature for 30 minutes. Bake at 350 degrees for 35 minutes or until set.

YIELD: 8 TO 10 SERVINGS

OVERNIGHT CHILE EGGS

8 eggs	2 cups milk
6 slices bread, crusts removed, cut into ½-inch squares	2 cups chopped green chilies
4 tablespoons butter, cut into ¼-inch squares	1½ cups grated Monterey Jack cheese or mixture of choice
	Salt and pepper to taste

Beat eggs in a large bowl. Add bread, butter, milk, chilies, Jack cheese, salt, and pepper. Mix well. Pour mixture into a well greased 13 x 9 x 2-inch baking dish. Cover and refrigerate at least 1 hour or overnight.

Bake, uncovered, at 300 degrees for 1 hour or until puffed and golden browned.

YIELD: 10 TO 12 SERVINGS

BLINTZ SOUFFLÉ

8-12	cheese or fruit filled blintzes	¼	cup orange juice
1	stick butter, melted	¼	cup sugar
6	eggs	¼	teaspoon salt
2	cups sour cream		
2	teaspoons vanilla		

Place frozen blintzes in a greased 2-quart casserole dish or 13 x 9 x 2-inch baking dish. Pour butter over blintzes. Beat eggs in a bowl. Add sour cream, vanilla, orange juice, sugar, and salt. Pour egg mixture over blintzes. Bake, uncovered, at 350 degrees for 45 minutes-1 hour or until golden browned.

YIELD: 10 TO 12 SERVINGS

The orange and vanilla create hit-the-spot flavors for the morning classic. May use blueberry or cherry or any fruity blintz.

SOUTHERN STYLE FRENCH TOAST CASSEROLE

The nutty-caramelized topping is on the bottom! A dependable crowd pleaser!

1	stick unsalted butter	1½	cups half & half
½	cup packed light brown sugar	1½	teaspoons cinnamon
½	cup pure maple syrup	1	teaspoon vanilla
1	cup chopped pecans	1	pound loaf challah bread
8	large eggs		

Heat butter, brown sugar and syrup in saucepan until butter melts. Pour mixture into a 13 x 9 x 2-inch baking dish. Sprinkle with pecans. Whisk together eggs, half & half, cinnamon, and vanilla. Layer bread slices over pecans. Pour egg mixture over bread. Cover and refrigerate overnight. Bake, uncovered, at 350 degrees for 40 minutes. Invert casserole onto a platter to serve.

YIELD: 8 TO 10 SERVINGS

CHOCOLATE CHIP MUFFINS

*Mini muffins or regular size, everyone loves a muffin
with the satisfying taste of a chocolate chip coming through.*

2½ cups all-purpose flour
3½ teaspoons baking powder
½ teaspoon salt
1½ sticks butter, softened
1 cup plus 1 tablespoon sugar, divided

2 large eggs
1½ teaspoons vanilla
¾ cup milk
1 cup semi-sweet chocolate chips

Preheat oven to 350 degrees. Grease muffin tins. Sift together flour, baking powder, and salt. Beat butter and 1 cup sugar with electric mixer until creamy. Scrape sides of bowl. Beat in one egg. Add second egg and vanilla. Beat well. Add half flour mixture and mix on low just until blended. Blend in milk. Mix in remaining flour mixture and chocolate chips. Fill muffin cups until almost full. Evenly sprinkle 1 tablespoon sugar over tops.

Bake at 350 degrees for 21-23 minutes or until golden browned and tester comes out clean. Cool 20 minutes in pan. Remove from muffin cups. Serve warm or room temperature.

YIELD: 8 TO 10 SERVINGS

EASY BREEZY BROCCOLI QUICHE

4 eggs
1 head broccoli, florets cooked and drained or 1 (10 ounce) package frozen
1 teaspoon salt
⅛ teaspoon pepper

¼ cup fresh mushrooms or jarred
¼ cup shredded Cheddar cheese or more to taste
¼ cup half & half or cream
1 (9-inch) frozen pie shell, thawed and unbaked

Preheat oven to 350 degrees. Beat eggs in a bowl. Add broccoli, salt, pepper, mushrooms, Cheddar cheese, and half & half. Pour filling into pie shell. Bake at 350 degrees for 45 minutes or until done.

YIELD: 6 TO 8 SERVINGS

BLUEBERRY-ORANGE MINI MUFFINS

These fruity fluffy muffins melt in your mouth!

1½ cups all-purpose flour

⅓ cup plus 2 tablespoons sugar, divided

2¼ teaspoons baking powder

¼ teaspoon salt

⅔ cup whole milk or soymilk

1 large egg, room temperature

1 teaspoon fine orange zest

½ teaspoon vanilla

⅔ cup fresh blueberries

6 tablespoons butter or margarine, cut into pieces

Preheat oven to 375 degrees. Combine flour, ⅓ cup sugar, baking powder, and salt. In a separate bowl, beat milk, egg, orange zest, and vanilla by hand. Stir in blueberries.

Add milk mixture and butter or margraine to flour mixture. Stir just until blended. Spoon batter into buttered muffin cups until mostly full. Sprinkle with 2 tablespoons sugar over tops. Bake at 375 degrees for 12-15 minutes or until golden browned and tester comes out clean. Cool on wire rack for 15 minutes. Serve warm or room temperature.

YIELD: 8 SERVINGS

CRUSTLESS SPINACH QUICHE

Crustless quiche makes for less carbs, but in the case of this quiche, not less taste!

1 (10 ounce) package frozen chopped spinach, cooked and well squeezed

3 eggs, beaten

1 (16 ounce) container cottage cheese

3 tablespoons all-purpose flour

1½ tablespoons butter, melted

1 cup shredded Cheddar cheese plus more for topping

Place spinach in a bowl. Add eggs, cottage cheese, flour, butter, and Cheddar cheese. Mix well. Pour filling into greased quiche plate. Top with Cheddar cheese. Bake at 350 degrees for 1 hour.

YIELD: 6 SERVINGS

CHEESE AND POBLANO PEPPER QUICHE

*Southerners are serious about their "heat" and
this French classic quiche can really pack some!*

1   garlic clove, minced
¾   teaspoon salt
6   large eggs
1   cup milk
½   cup heavy cream
2   teaspoons grated white onion

½   teaspoon pepper
1   (9-inch) deep dish pie shell, unbaked
1   pound poblano chilies, roasted and peeled
1   (8 ounce) package shredded Monterey Jack cheese

Preheat oven to 375 degrees. Whisk together garlic, salt, eggs, milk, cream, onion, and pepper. Pour filling into pie shell. Remove seeds and ribs of chilies and pat dry. Sprinkle Jack cheese and chilies over filling. Bake at 375 degrees for 50-60 minutes. Cool for 20 minutes before serving.

YIELD: 6 TO 8 SERVINGS

SALMON QUICHE

1   onion, diced
3-4 tablespoons vegetable oil
3   (6 ounce) cans boneless skinless salmon
¾   cup cornflake crumbs plus extra for topping

2   tablespoons chopped fresh parsley
1   cup soymilk or coffee rich
1   (9-inch) deep dish pie shell, unbaked

Sauté onion in oil until slightly caramelized. Combine onion, salmon, crumbs, parsley, and soymilk. Pour filling into pie shell. Sprinkle cornflake crumbs on top. Bake at 350 degrees for 1 hour to 1 hour, 15 minutes.

YIELD: 6 TO 8 SERVINGS

TUNA QUICHE

2   (6 ounce) cans tuna, drained
¾   cup mayonnaise
½   onion, finely chopped
3   eggs, beaten

¾   cup soymilk or coffee rich
    Dash of garlic powder
1   (9-inch) deep dish pie shell,
     unbaked

Combine tuna, mayonnaise, onion, eggs, soymilk, and garlic powder. Pour filling into pie crust or tart shells. Bake at 350 degrees for 45 minutes.

YIELD: 6 TO 8 SERVINGS

Browning onions before adding to recipes will enhance their flavor.

SIMPLE SWEET NOODLE PUDDING

A creamy Jewish classic with a sweet crunchy topping!

TOPPING
1   stick butter, melted
½   cup sugar

⅔   cup graham cracker crumbs

TOPPING

Combine butter, sugar and cracker crumbs.

NOODLES
1   package noodles
6   tablespoons butter, softened
6   egg yolks
1   cup sugar
6   ounces cream cheese, softened

1   (16 ounce) container cottage
     cheese
¼   cup sour cream
6   egg whites

NOODLES

Cook noodles according to package directions. Add butter to hot noodles. Blend egg yolks, sugar, cream cheese, cottage cheese, and sour cream. Pour mixture over noodles. Whip egg whites. Fold into noodles. Pour noodle mixture into a greased 13 x 9 x 2-inch baking dish. Sprinkle topping over noodles. Bake at 350 degrees for 1 hour.

YIELD: 10 TO 12 SERVINGS

FRESH CORN, TOMATO AND BASIL GRATIN

During the summer months when the tomatoes, corn and basil are growing everywhere, this dish is so satisfying. It can be a meal or a side and it is full of flavor!

1½ pounds sweet red or yellow tomatoes, cut crosswise into ½-inch slices
2 teaspoons salt, divided
1 teaspoon pepper, divided
4 cups fresh corn kernels (6-8 ears)

1 cup whole milk
½ cup heavy cream
2 cups fresh bread crumbs
½ cup fresh basil, chopped
¼ cup grated Parmesan cheese
6 tablespoons unsalted butter, cut into small pieces

Arrange tomato slices on a rack set in a shallow baking pan. Sprinkle with 1 teaspoon salt and ½ teaspoon pepper. Drain for 30 minutes.

Combine corn, milk, cream, and ¼ teaspoon salt in a saucepan. Bring to simmer over high heat. Reduce heat and simmer, partially covered, 5 minutes until corn is tender.

Place oven rack in upper third of oven. Preheat to 375 degrees. Combine bread crumbs, basil, Parmesan cheese, ¾ teaspoon salt, and ½ teaspoon pepper in a bowl. Arrange one-third tomato slices in a baking dish. Cover with one-third crumb mixture and dot with one-third butter. Spoon one-half corn mixture over crumbs. Repeat layering of tomatoes, crumbs, butter, and remaining corn. Top with remaining crumbs and dot with butter. Bake, uncovered, at 375 degrees for 40-45 minutes or until golden browned and bubbly. Cool on rack for 15 minutes.

YIELD: 10 TO 12 SERVINGS

CHEESE GRITS CASSEROLE

This creative concept gives gourmet glamour to Dixie's love affair with grits.

1 cup grits
¼-½ teaspoon pepper
3 dashes of Worcestershire sauce

1½ pounds Cheddar cheese, grated
1 egg

Cook grits according to package directions. Stir in pepper, Worcestershire sauce, Cheddar cheese, and egg into hot grits. Pour mixture into a casserole dish. Bake at 375 degrees for 45-50 minutes.

YIELD: 4 TO 6 SERVINGS

SWEET ONION SOUFFLÉ

This creamy dish is a delicious addition to a vegetable plate or paired with fish.

2	tablespoons butter	3	large eggs, beaten
5	medium sweet onions, chopped	1¼	cups Parmesan cheese, divided
2	cups fresh bread cubes	1	teaspoon salt
1	(12 ounce) can fat free evaporated milk		

Melt butter in a large skillet. Sauté onion 10-15 minutes or until tender and almost caramelized. Transfer onion to a bowl. Add bread cubes to bowl. Stir in milk, eggs, 1 cup Parmesan cheese, and salt. Pour mixture into a lightly greased 1½-quart soufflé or baking dish. Sprinkle with ¼ cup Parmesan cheese. Bake at 350 degrees for 25 minutes or until set.

YIELD: 6 TO 8 SERVINGS

TUNA FISH SANDWICH CASSEROLE

4	cans tuna	¼	celery stalk, chopped (optional)
4	hard-boiled eggs	2	loaves of sliced white bread (need to make about 14-16 sandwices)
4	tablespoons pickle relish		
1	generous cup mayonnaise	14-16	eggs, well beaten
½	teaspoon salt	2	cups shredded Cheddar cheese
	Dash of pepper		

Mix together tuna, hard-boiled eggs, pickle relish, mayonnaise, salt and pepper (and chopped celery). Cut the crust off the white bread. Make sandwiches with tuna fish salad. Then cut the sandwiches diagonally, then in half to form 4 triangles per sandwich.

Spray a 9 x 13-inch dish with non-stick cooking spray. Line up sandwich triangles into two rows. Line the peaks up as tight as possible. Beat together 1 egg per sandwich and pour over sandwiches. Sprinkle the 2 cups of Cheddar cheese over the top. Refrigerate overnight. Bake for 25-30 minutes in a 350 degree oven.

FRUIT WITH SOUR CREAM SAUCE

The sauce's velvety smoothness is a perfect playmate for the juicy fruit.
This can be made with non-dairy sour cream!

SOUR CREAM SAUCE

5⅓ tablespoons butter, softened	½ teaspoon lemon juice
1 cup powdered sugar	¼ teaspoon vanilla
½ cup sour cream	

SOUR CREAM SAUCE

Beat butter and powdered sugar with electric mixer until smooth. Beat in sour cream, lemon juice and vanilla until creamy. Cover and refrigerate until ready to serve or up to 8 hours.

FRUIT

⅓ cup sugar	1 banana, sliced
1 cup water	1 Granny Smith apple, chopped
6 fresh mint leaves	1 cup seedless green grapes
1 (8 ounce) can pineapple chunks, drained	1 cup strawberries, sliced
	Mint sprigs for garnish

FRUIT

Combine sugar, water, and mint in a saucepan. Bring to boil. Cook and stir 4-5 minutes until mixture reaches a syrup consistency. Discard mint and cool completely.

Combine pineapple, banana, apple, grapes, and strawberries in a large bowl. Pour syrup mixture over fruit and gently toss to coat. Cover and refrigerate at least 1 hour. Before serving, pour sour cream sauce over fruit. Garnish with mint sprigs.

YIELD: 8 SERVINGS

STICKY SWEET ROLL CAKE

Sweet and sticky like yummy sweet rolls!

1 **(18 ounce) package yellow cake mix**	1 **cup packed brown sugar**
1 **stick butter**	1 **cup chopped pecans**
¼ **cup water**	1⅓ **cups coconut**

Preheat oven to 375 degrees. Prepare cake mix according to package directions. Melt butter in 13 x 9 x 2-inch baking dish. Stir in water, brown sugar, pecans, and coconut. Mix well and spread evenly in dish. Pour cake batter over top. Bake at 375 degrees for 45-55 minutes. Cool 5 minutes.

YIELD: 10 TO 12 SERVINGS

YOGURT PEAR PARFAIT

Looks pretty and tastes great. A perfect winter fruit dessert for brunch!

4 **firm ripe pears, peeled, cored and quartered**	¼ **cup packed light brown sugar**
2 **teaspoons lemon juice**	1 **cup granola, divided**
3 **tablespoons butter**	1⅓ **cups vanilla flavored yogurt**
1 **teaspoon cinnamon**	¼ **cup finely chopped crystallized ginger**
1 **pinch of ground allspice**	

Toss pears with lemon juice in a bowl. Heat a large skillet over high heat. Melt butter in skillet. Add pears. Cook and stir about 3-4 minutes or until golden browned. Stir in cinnamon and allspice. Add brown sugar. Cook 2-3 minutes until pears are tender and juices have formed a syrup consistency. Remove from heat.

Parfaits may be assembled while pears are warm or cool. Place 2 tablespoons granola in bottom of four parfaits glasses. Add ⅓ cup yogurt to each glass. Divide caramelized pears among four glasses. Top each with 2 tablespoons granola. Sprinkle with crystallized ginger. May refrigerate but best served immediately

YIELD: 4 SERVINGS

WORLD FAMOUS GRANOLA

This recipe was such a family secret. It was gifted to a family friend for a high school graduation gift. Kept a secret for many years, it has finally been released for the publishing.

7 cups quick oats	1½ cups dry roasted peanuts
1½ cups packed brown sugar	1 cup almonds
7 cups crunch oat bran cereal	1 cup vegetable oil
1½ cups wheat germ	1 cup honey
1 (7 ounce) package shredded coconut	1 tablespoon vanilla
⅔ cup sunflower seeds	2 cups raisins
	1½ cups dates (optional)

Place oats on a large ungreased roasting pan. Bake at 350 degrees for 10 minutes. Combine oats, brown sugar, cereal, wheat germ, coconut, sunflower seeds, peanuts, and almonds. In a separate bowl, blend oil, honey, and vanilla. Pour sauce over dry ingredients and toss to coat well. Bake at 350 degrees for 30-35 minutes, stirring often. Add raisins and dates during last 10 minutes of baking. Cool and stir until crumbly.

YIELD: 15 TO 20 SERVINGS

Pasta, Grains & Rice

Love is the most important ingredient in all recipes.
Here's to my favorite chef of all...my mother,
*Marilyn Pollack...*who taught me to love cooking.
By *Julie and Marty Belz*

Growing up in Cape Girardeau, Missouri, where there were not enough men to have a minyan of ten Jewish men except on the High Holy Days, Julie Pollack Belz developed a unique determination to honor her heritage. Although the Jewish community was miniscule, the Pollack family made sure to have weekly Sabbath dinners, frequently entertaining the few Jewish travelers who passed their way. Now living in Memphis, Julie does not have that same problem. A vivacious hostess, she loves sharing her traditional Jewish comfort food recipes, including her "Simple Sweet Noodle Pudding." "I wanted to take the foods of my Jewish heritage, from the rural town I grew up in, and make them fresh and exciting for my Sabbath table today." Just as lively as she is welcoming, Julie proves that when it comes to kosher cooking, all you need is a little tradition and someone to share it with.

DOWN HOME MAC & CHEESE

4	tablespoons butter		Salt and pepper to taste
¼	cup all-purpose flour	1	pound elbow macaroni, cooked
1½	cups milk		al dente and drained
½	cup heavy cream		Bread crumbs (optional)
2½	cups shredded Cheddar cheese, divided		

Preheat oven to 350 degrees. Melt butter in a heavy saucepan. Whisk in flour to make a roux. Gradually whisk in milk and cream. Bring to simmer. Cook and whisk 1 minute until smooth. Add 2 cups Cheddar cheese, salt and pepper. Whisk until smooth. Stir in macaroni. Pour mixture into a shallow 2-quart baking dish. Bake, uncovered, at 350 degrees for 20-25 minutes or until bubbly and golden browned. Top with ½ cup Cheddar cheese and bread crumbs during last 5 minutes of baking. Cool 10 minutes before serving.

YIELD: 6 SERVINGS

Pasta, Grains & Rice

PASTA PRIMAVERA

3	tablespoons olive oil, divided	½	cup frozen peas
3	tablespoons butter, divided	¾	cup white wine
5-6	green onions, mostly white, finely chopped	2	teaspoons dried dill
3	carrots, julienne cut	1	teaspoon salt
1	yellow pepper, julienne cut	½	teaspoon pepper
1	(4 ounce) jar roasted red pepper, drained and chopped	½	cup grated Parmesan cheese
12	grape tomatoes, halved or 2 tomatoes, chopped	1	pound angel hair pasta, cooked al dente

Heat 2 tablespoons oil and 2 tablespoons butter in a skillet over medium heat. Add green onion, carrot, and yellow pepper. Cover and cook 5-7 minutes until tender. Add remaining oil and butter. Stir in red pepper, tomatoes, and peas. Add wine, dill, salt, and pepper. Mix well. Reduce heat and cook 10-15 minutes or until vegetables are tender and wine is reduced. Stir in Parmesan cheese. Pour mixture over pasta.

YIELD: 8 SERVINGS

May use different or additional vegetables, like broccoli or sweet red pepper. Cook crisp vegetables first then add softer vegetables.

It is best to serve cooked past immediately, but it can be held for a little while if needed. Drain the cooked pasta and immerse it into a bowl of cold water to stop the cooking process. Mix the pasta in the cold water to be sure it is completely cooled. Drain it again and toss it with oil to keep it from sticking and clumping. When you are ready to serve the pasta, immerse it in warm or simmering water to reheat it and serve innediately!

MEMPHIS' SPECIAL PASTA

This recipe is inspired by a treasured recipe from a landmark restaurant in Memphis.

8	ounces thin spaghetti, cooked	1	package imitation crab cut in bite-sized pieces
1½	sticks butter		Parmesan cheese
1	tablespoon minced garlic		Black peper
8	ounces mushrooms, sliced		

Melt butter in a skillet. Sauté garlic for 1-2 minutes. Add mushrooms and sauté until brown. Add crab to skillet until heated through and pour over pasta. Add Parmesan and black pepper to taste.

The key to this recipe is the simplicity and richness of the garlic butter sauce — feel free to add onions, peppers, capers — be adventurous!

LASAGNA ROLLS

A tasty twist on an Italian classic! It is easier to serve than traditional lasagna.

SAUCE

2	tablespoons unsalted butter	¼	teaspoon salt
4	teaspoons all-purpose flour	⅛	teaspoon pepper
1¼	cups whole milk		Pinch of ground nutmeg

SAUCE

Melt butter in a heavy medium saucepan over medium-low heat. Whisk in flour for 3 minutes. Whisk in milk. Bring to simmer, whisking constantly for 3 minutes until thickened and smooth. Add salt, pepper, and nutmeg. Pour sauce into a greased 13 x 9 x 2-inch baking dish.

ROLLS

1	(15 ounce) container whole milk ricotta cheese	¾	tablespoon salt
1	(10 ounce) package frozen chopped spinach, thawed and squeezed dry	½	teaspoon pepper
		2	tablespoons olive oil
1	cup plus 2 tablespoons grated Parmesan cheese, divided	12	lasagna noodles, uncooked
		2	cups *DonPepino* pizza sauce, divided
1	large egg, beaten	1	cup shredded mozzarella cheese

ROLLS

Preheat oven to 450 degrees. Whisk together ricotta cheese, spinach, 1 cup Parmesan cheese, egg, salt, and pepper until blended. Add oil to large pot of salted boiling water. Cook noodles until al dente. Drain and arrange in single layer on a baking sheet. Arrange four noodles on a work surface. Spread 3 tablespoons ricotta cheese mixture over each noodle. Roll up noodle jelly-roll fashion. Place rolls seam side down over sauce in baking dish without touching each other. Repeat with remaining noodles and cheese mixture.

Spoon 1 cup pizza sauce over rolls. Sprinkle with mozzarella cheese and 2 tablespoons Parmesan cheese. Cover tightly with foil. Bake at 450 degrees for 20 minutes until bubbly. Remove foil and bake an additional 15 minutes or until golden browned. Cool 10 minutes. Heat remaining 1 cup pizza sauce and serve on the side.

YIELD: 8 TO 10 SERVINGS

The base sauce for this pasta recipe is béchamel sauce or white sauce. It is considered one of the "mohter sauces" in French cuisine and provides creaminess to the dish.

SPICY LEMON PASTA

Lemons and jalapeños provide a fresh flavor with a kick!

1   pound spaghetti, fettuccini or linguini

3   tablespoons olive oil, divided

Zest of 2 lemons

3   garlic cloves, minced

2   jalapeño peppers, seeded and thinly sliced

Juice of 2 lemons

1½ cups frozen peas, thawed

1   teaspoon kosher salt

⅛   teaspoon pepper

⅓   cup grated Parmesan cheese

Cook pasta according to package directions. Heat 2 tablespoons oil in a large skillet. Add lemon zest, garlic and jalapeño pepper. Cook 4-5 minutes until lightly browned. Add pasta, 1 tablespoon oil, lemon juice, peas, salt, and pepper. Heat for 3-4 minutes. Add Parmesan cheese and toss to coat.

YIELD: 6 SERVINGS

May substitute canned jalapeños or crushed red pepper for fresh jalapeños.

ITALIAN CHEESE TOASTS

6   (½-inch) slices Italian bread

¼   cup part skim or fat free ricotta cheese

1   tablespoon grated Parmesan cheese

1   tablespoon fresh finely chopped basil

⅛   teaspoon lemon zest

Pinch of salt

Preheat oven to 400 degrees. Place bread slices on a baking sheet. Bake for 4 minutes until golden browned. Combine ricotta cheese, Parmesan cheese, basil, lemon zest, and salt. Remove bread from oven. Spread cheese mixture on bread. May return to oven to melt cheese.

YIELD: 6 SERVINGS

LINGUINE WITH TUNA, CAPERS AND RAISINS

The delicate raisins and capers give sweet and sour little bursts of flavor!

1	pound linguine	2	(6 ounce) cans tuna, drained
½	cup extra virgin olive oil	⅓	cup capers in brine, drained and rinsed
1	cup chopped onion	¾	cup golden raisins
3	garlic cloves, finely chopped	½	cup chopped flat leaf parsley
½	teaspoon salt		
¼	teaspoon pepper		

Cook pasta in a 6 to 8-quart stockpot of salted boiling water until al dente. Reserve 1 cup pasta water. Drain pasta well. Heat oil in a 12-inch skillet over high heat until hot but not smoking. Sauté onion and garlic, stirring occasionally, 6-8 minutes until golden browned. Stir in salt, pepper, tuna, capers, raisins, parsley, and reserved pasta water. Mix well. Add tuna mixture to pasta and toss to combine. Serve immediately.

YIELD: 6 SERVINGS

FETTUCCINI WITH MUSHROOM ALFREDO SAUCE

Mushrooms in creamy Alfredo sauce.
Don't count the calories on this one. It is a splurge!

4	tablespoons butter	1	cup grated Parmesan cheese
½	pound mushrooms, chopped (portabella, button, or cremini)	1	teaspoon coarsely ground pepper
3	garlic cloves, minced	½	teaspoon salt
1	cup heavy cream	2	tablespoons chopped parsley
1	cup milk	1	(12 ounce) package fettuccini, cooked al dente

Melt butter in a large saucepan over medium heat. Sauté mushrooms and garlic 5-6 minutes or until tender. Stir in cream and milk. Bring to boil over medium heat. Reduce heat and simmer, whisking constantly for 10 minutes. Stir in Parmesan cheese, pepper and salt. Stir constantly until cheese melts and mixture thickens. Add parsley. Serve over hot pasta.

YIELD: 6 SERVINGS

ROASTED TOMATOES OVER ANGEL HAIR PASTA

*The thing that is great about this pasta is that it is light,
not saucy, but the roasted tomatoes are full of flavor.*

- 2 pounds ripe plum tomatoes, cut lengthwise into ¼-inch slices
- 3 large garlic cloves, minced
- ⅓ cup olive oil
- 1 tablespoon dried basil
- 1 teaspoon sugar
- 1 teaspoon Tabasco sauce
- Salt and pepper to taste
- ¾ cup grated Parmesan cheese
- ¾ pound angel hair pasta
- Pepper to taste
- Parmesan cheese for garnish

Preheat oven to 450 degrees. Gently combine tomatoes, garlic, oil, basil, sugar, Tabasco, salt, pepper, and Parmesan cheese in a large bowl. Spoon mixture into a single layer on a large, low-sided, non-stick baking sheet. Bake at 450 degrees for 30 minutes or until tomatoes are tender and edges charred. Transfer to a large bowl. Cook pasta until al dente. Drain well and immediately toss with tomato mixture. Sprinkle with pepper. Serve with Parmesan cheese.

YIELD: 6 SERVINGS

SHELBY COUNTY PASTA SHELLS

Using non-fat cottage cheese and an egg white cuts the fat for this pasta dish!

- 1 (10 ounce) package frozen spinach, thawed and drained
- 1½ cups grated mozzarella cheese
- 1½ cups non-fat cottage cheese
- 1 egg white
- 1½ tablespoons grated Parmesan cheese
- ½ teaspoon ground nutmeg
- 16 pasta shells
- 1 (15 ounce) can Don Pepino pizza sauce

Combine spinach, mozzarella cheese, cottage cheese, egg white, Parmesan cheese, and nutmeg. Spoon mixture into pasta shells. Arrange shells in a greased 13 x 9 x 2-inch baking dish. Pour pizza sauce over shells. Cover with foil. Bake at 375 degrees for 30-40 minutes.

YIELD: 6 TO 8 SERVINGS

SOUTHERN BELLE PEPPER PESTO LINGUINI

*The roasted peppers and fresh flavors of the garlic
and cilantro are processed into a sauce that is rich in flavor, not fat!*

1 large yellow pepper, seeded and cut into 6 pieces	2 tablespoons lemon juice, divided
1 large sweet red pepper, seeded and cut into 6 pieces	⅓ cup olive oil
6 large mushrooms	1 teaspoon salt
5 garlic cloves	½ teaspoon ground cumin
2 tablespoons capers	½ teaspoon pepper
1½ cups cilantro, stems removed	1 pound linguine, cooked al dente
	Parmesan cheese (optional)

Place pepper, mushrooms, garlic, capers, and cilantro on a baking sheet. Drizzle with 1 tablespoon lemon juice and toss to coat. Roast at 400 degrees for 25-30 minutes or until peppers are almost blackened and mushrooms are tender. Remove from oven and cover with foil. Let stand for 10 minutes to loosen skin on pepper.

Peel and discard pepper skin. Combine pepper, mushroom, garlic, capers, and cilantro mixture in a food processor or blender. Add 1 tablespoon lemon juice, oil, salt, cumin, and pepper. Process until smooth, scraping down sides. Serve sauce over hot pasta. Sprinkle with Parmesan cheese.

YIELD: 6 SERVINGS

CLASSIC GARLIC BREAD

2 teaspoons finely chopped garlic	1 tablespoon extra virgin olive oil
¼ teaspoon salt	2 tablespoons finely chopped flat leaf parsley
4 tablespoons unsalted butter, softened	1 (15 x 3 ½-inch) loaf Italian bread

Preheat oven to 350 degrees. Mash garlic into salt to form a paste.
Blend garlic paste, butter, and oil until smooth. Stir in parsley.
Cut bread diagonally, without cutting through bottom, into 1-inch thick slices.
Spread butter between slices. Wrap bread in foil. Bake at 350 degrees on
middle rack for 15 minutes. Open foil and bake an additional 5 minutes.

CAPELLINI WITH ITALIAN SPICED TUNA, MUSHROOMS AND ARTICHOKES

Full flavored-use plenty of spices! Great for leftover tuna steaks.

2	tablespoons olive oil		1	teaspoon dried basil
1	medium onion, chopped		1	teaspoon dried oregano
2	garlic cloves, minced		½	teaspoon celery seed
8	mushrooms, thinly sliced		1	pound capellini
1	(14 ounce) can artichoke hearts, drained and quartered		4	quarts water
			⅓	cup chopped parsley
2	(6 ounce) cans solid white tuna in water, drained		⅓	cup grated Parmesan cheese

Heat oil in a 12-inch skillet. Sauté onion, garlic and mushroom 10 minutes or until tender but not browned. Add artichokes. Break tuna into bite size pieces and add to skillet. Stir in basil, oregano and celery seed. Cook for 5 minutes to heat tuna and artichokes. Bring salted water to boil. Cook capellini 7 minutes until al dente. Drain well. Place in a serving bowl. Add tuna mixture and toss to coat. Top with parsley and Parmesan cheese.

YIELD: 6 SERVINGS

SPAGHETTI WITH GARLIC AND OIL

Ridiculously easy and delicious.

⅓	cup olive oil	Salt and pepper to taste
8	garlic cloves, minced	Grated Parmesan cheese
1	pound spaghetti, cooked al dente	for garnish

Heat oil in a skillet over medium heat. Add garlic and cook until golden browned but not burnt. Remove from heat. Add pasta and toss to combine. Sprinkle with salt and pepper. Top with Parmesan cheese.

YIELD: 4 SERVINGS

COUNTY'S BEST ZITI

*Everyone loves a pasta dish which can be served
to a crowd and comes out perfect every time. Well, this ziti is it!*

1 (12 ounce) container ricotta cheese	2 tablespoons chopped fresh parsley
2 eggs, beaten	1 pound ziti, cooked al dente
¾ cup grated Parmesan cheese, divided	3 cans *Don Pepino* pizza sauce, divided
½ teaspoon salt	1 (8 ounce) block mozzarella cheese, cut into ½-inch cubes
¼ teaspoon pepper	

Preheat oven to 350 degrees. Combine ricotta cheese, eggs, ½ cup Parmesan cheese, salt, pepper, and parsley. Mix well. Toss ziti with 2 cups pizza sauce. Spread half pasta in a 13 x 9 x 2-inch baking dish. Top with ricotta cheese mixture and half mozzarella cubes. Top with remaining ziti, 1 cup pizza sauce, mozzarella cubes and ¼ cup Parmesan cheese. Bake at 350 degrees for 30-35 minutes or until heated through and cheese is bubbly and lightly browned.

YIELD: 6 TO 8 SERVINGS

NANA'S BAKED SPAGHETTI

No fuss, no muss, and the kids will gobble it down! The grown-ups like it too!

8 ounces spaghetti, cooked al dente	Pinch of salt
1 (10¾ ounce) can tomato soup	2 tablespoons butter, cut into small pieces, reserve some for top
1 (8 ounce) package shredded Cheddar cheese, reserve some for top	

Preheat oven to 350 degrees. Combine spaghetti, tomato soup, Cheddar cheese, salt, and butter. Pour mixture into a greased round casserole dish. Sprinkle with Cheddar cheese and butter. Bake at 350 degrees for 30 minutes or until cheese melts.

YIELD: 4 SERVINGS

The Perfect Weeknight meal: Nana's Baked Spaghetti, Salmon Loaf and steamed broccoli.

BARLEY PILAF

A hearty tummy warmer on chilly days!
This is a great accompaniment to fish or chicken.

1½ sticks margarine, divided
1 pound mushrooms
1 large onion, finely chopped

2 cups barley
5½ cups chicken broth
Salt and pepper to taste

Heat 4 tablespoons of margarine in skillet. Sauté mushrooms 5 minutes until browned. Add 1 stick margarine and onion. Cook until tender. Add barley and cook until lightly browned. Combine mushrooms and barley mixture in a 3-quart casserole dish. Pour in 3 cups broth. Cover and bake at 350 degrees 30 minutes.

Add 2 cups broth to casserole. Cover and bake for 1 hour. If barley is dry, add ½ cup broth and bake, covered, an additional 20 minutes. If barley is not dry, uncover and bake 15 minutes until browned.

Pilaf may stay covered in the oven for 30 minutes or reheated. If freezing, after first 30 minutes of baking, cool pilaf, cover and freeze.

YIELD: 6 TO 8 SERVINGS

BARLEY AND MIXED MUSHROOM CASSEROLE

High in fiber, bursting with taste!

2 tablespoons margarine
2 medium onions, finely diced
1 carrot, finely chopped
1 stalk celery, thinly sliced
¾ pound sliced mushrooms
   (4½ cups combination button, cremini, portabella or shiitake)

1½ cups barley
1½ teaspoons ground thyme
¾ teaspoon salt
¾ teaspoon pepper
4½ cups hot vegetable broth

Melt margarine in skillet. Add onions, carrot, celery, mushrooms, barley, thyme, salt, and pepper. Sauté for 10 minutes. Add vegetable broth. Put in 13 x 9 x 2-inch baking dish. Cover tightly and cook 1-1¼ hours.

YIELD: 4 TO 6 SERVINGS

YERUSHALMI KUGEL

Kugels have been made for more than 800 years. The word "kugel" comes from the Germanic root meaning "ball" or "globe," and the Yiddish name likely originated as a reference to the round, puffy shape of the original dishes.

Jerusalem kugels are distinguished from other kugels by their combination of caramelized sugar and pepper.

4¼	cups water	2	teaspoons salt
¾	teaspoon pepper	3	tablespoons vegetable oil
3	tablespoons packed brown sugar	1	pound fine noodles
1	cup sugar	2	eggs, beaten
1	stick margarine		

Bring water, pepper, brown sugar, sugar, margarine, salt, and oil to boil. Add noodles. Turn off heat and let stand for 10 minutes. Quickly add eggs and pour into a 13 x 9 x 2-inch or 8 x 8 x 2-inch baking dish (for thicker kugel). Bake at 350 degrees for 45 minutes.

YIELD: 10 SERVINGS

ORIENTAL RICE AND NOODLES

This delicious casserole is great with an Asian-style main dish but also works well with an all-American meal.

1	cup rice	1	teaspoon powdered chicken bouillon (parve)
¾	cup fine noodles	4	cups boiling water
1	cup orzo	1	tablespoon soy sauce
6	tablespoons margarine		Salt, pepper and garlic powder to taste
1	(1¼ ounce) package dry onion soup mix	1	(8 ounce) can sliced mushrooms, drained

Fry rice, noodles and orzo in margarine until golden browned. Dissolve onion soup mix and chicken bouillon in boiling water in a large bowl. Add rice mixture. Stir in soy sauce, salt, pepper, garlic powder, and mushrooms. Mix well. Pour mixture into a greased 13 x 9 x 2-inch baking dish. Bake at 350 degrees for 30-45 minutes or until liquid is absorbed.

YIELD: 8 TO 10 SERVINGS

CHEESY NOODLE CASSEROLE

1	pound medium noodles		1	pint cottage cheese
1½	sticks butter		1	cup milk
6	eggs		1	tablespoon salt
¼	pound Cheddar cheese, grated		1	tablespoon sugar
1	pint sour cream			Dash pepper

TOPPING

½	stick melted butter		1	cup cornflake crumbs
¼	pound Cheddar cheese, grated			

Cook noodles and drain Melt 1½ sticks of butter over noodles. Mix in the next 8 ingredients with noodles. Spray a 9 x 13-inch baking dish with non-stick cooking spray. Pour noodle mixture into dish. Mix together topping and spread evenly over the top. Bake in 350 degree oven for 1 hour. It should be sizzling!

SWEET RICE PUDDING

4	eggs, beaten			Pinch of salt
3	cups soymilk or 2 cups soymilk and 1 cup water		⅓	cup sugar
1	(3 ounce) package instant vanilla pudding mix		1	teaspoon vanilla
			3	cups cooked rice
1	stick margarine, melted			Sugar and cinnamon to taste

Combine eggs, soymilk, pudding mix, margarine, salt, sugar, and vanilla. Stir into rice and mix well. Pour mixture into a greased 3-quart casserole dish. Sprinkle with sugar and cinnamon. Bake at 350 degrees for 1 hour.

YIELD: 4 SERVINGS

Meats

"Everything derives from women." Midrash:Breshit Rabbah 17

To: the most important women in my life:

Lisa ■ *Talia* ■ *Elaina* ■ *Ariana* ■ *Leah "Bubbie" Kaufman* ■ *Diane "Didi" Wruble*

by *Seth Kaufman*

When one thinks of Memphis-style cooking, sisters and best friends Diane Leach Wruble and Joan Leach Baum certainly come to mind. They share everything: backyards, vacations, and holiday meals. Most of all, following a long line of Memphis entertainers that dates back to the 1900s, they share a love of entertaining.

Whether it is the new family in town or simply a weekend visitor looking for good kosher, Southern cooking, everyone feels at home around the Wruble and Baum tables, which are often set for up to fifty guests! The food is certainly a draw, as the sisters provide some of the best Sabbath meals south of the Mason-Dixon Line. They are known for their eclectic menus of classic Jewish and Southern-style dishes. However, the real sweetness of their meals comes from the welcoming nature of these true Southern belles. Diane's classic grace and Joan's cheerful energy are evident whenever they host. Their love of their heritage, combined with their timeless hospitality, make it well worth the trip to get a real taste of Southern-style cooking and generous hospitality. We are lucky that Diane and Joan were raised with the following adage: "You not only share your table, but you share your recipes."

RASPBERRY-PECAN CRUSTED LAMB CHOPS

3   pounds lamb chops
    Salt and pepper to taste
6   tablespoons raspberry jam
¼   cup Dijon mustard

¾   cup finely chopped pecans
6   tablespoons minced Italian parsley
¾   cup homemade bread crumbs
4   tablespoons margarine, melted

Preheat oven to 425 degrees. Sprinkle lamb chops with salt and pepper. Whisk together jam and mustard until smooth. Combine pecans, parsley, and bread crumbs in a separate bowl. Spread jam mixture over chops. Dredge in bread crumbs. Place in a well greased baking dish. Drizzle each chop with margarine. Roast at 425 degrees for 15 minutes. Gently turn and roast an additional 15 minutes until golden browned.

YIELD: 6 TO 8 SERVINGS

RED BEANS AND RICE

A great alternative to cholent that can be kicked up by increasing the spices. This recipe has been known to put a pregnant Sabbath guest into labor!

1   pound red beans
1   large red onion, chopped
1   bunch green onions, chopped
1   cup chopped Italian parsley
2   large garlic cloves, chopped
1   tablespoon hickory flavored salt
½   teaspoon crushed red pepper
1   teaspoon pepper
½   cup sugar

    Dash of Tabasco sauce
¼   teaspoon dried oregano
¼   teaspoon dried thyme
1   tablespoon Worcestershire sauce
1   (15 ounce) can *Don Pepino* pizza sauce
1   pound Italian veal sausage, sliced
1   pound ground beef
    Hot cooked rice

Combine beans, red onion, green onion, parsley, garlic, salt, red pepper, pepper, sugar, Tabasco, oregano, thyme, Worcestershire sauce, pizza sauce, sausage, and beef in a large crock pot. Pour in water to cover. Cook on low until meat is tender, 3-5 hours. Serve over hot rice.

YIELD: 8 TO 10 SERVINGS

SLOW-COOKED TENDER ROAST

*Liquid is especially important when cooking meat in a crockpot.
This recipe uses wine, soy sauce, and the natural juice of onions as
a more flavorful alternative to water for rich and hearty gravy.*

A great alternative for the Sabbath lunch instead of cholent.

SAUCE
1   teaspoon Dijon mustard

½   cup packed brown sugar

1   cup ketchup

White vinegar to taste

SAUCE

Blend mustard, brown sugar, ketchup, and white vinegar to desired consistency.

MEAT
2   onions, sliced

3-5 pounds roast

½   bottle red wine

1   tablespoon soy sauce

1   (1¼ ounce) package dry onion
     soup mix

MEAT

Place onions in bottom of crockpot. Place roast on top. Pour in wine, soy sauce, onion soup mix, and enough water to cover meat. Cook on low overnight.

Shred and chop meat and some onions. Pour sauce over meat. May serve as BBQ beef with buns.

YIELD: 12 SERVINGS

In the South our barbeque sandwiches go hand in hand with a helping of our Memphis' Favorite Cole Slaw.

SOUL FOOD STEW...
A SOUTHERN CHOLENT

A dish born out of observance of the Sabbath, some believe cholent was brought to America by the Pilgrims, who adopted it after spending time with the Jews of Holland before sailing to the New World.

1	large onion, chopped	¼	cup barbeque sauce
1-2	large potatoes, diced	1	tablespoon salt
1	pound barley, uncooked	1	tablespoon garlic powder
1	pound beef, cubed	1	tablespoon onion powder
1	pound Polish sausage or hot dogs	½	tablespoon pepper
½	pound kishke		

Combine onion, potato, barley, beef, sausage, kishke, barbeque sauce, salt, garlic powder, onion powder, and pepper in a crockpot. Cover with 4-6 cups water. Put in crockpot and cook on low overnight.

YIELD: 8 TO 10 SERVINGS

LONDON BROIL

2	tablespoons soy sauce	1-2	garlic cloves, minced
1	tablespoon minced ginger	1	teaspoon pepper
1	tablespoon slivered lime zest	1	tablespoon brown sugar
2	tablespoons vegetable oil	3-4	pound London broil, flank steak

Combine soy sauce, ginger, lime zest, oil, garlic, pepper, and brown sugar in a baking dish. Add meat to marinade and turn to coat. Marinate overnight. Remove from marinade. Grill 10-15 minutes per side depending on the thickness. Place meat in a clean baking dish and cook at 325 degrees for 15 minutes or to desired degree of doneness. Thinly slice meat across grain. Should be pink on inside and seared on outside.

YIELD: 6 TO 8 SERVINGS

Meats

GRANDMA'S SWEET AND SOUR BRISKET

Double the recipe and plan to freeze half for later use!

All-purpose flour for dusting	**½ cup vinegar**
6-7 pound beef brisket	**1 cup ketchup**
3 onions, sliced	**1 cup water**
1 garlic clove, minced	**1 tablespoon salt**
¼ cup packed brown sugar	**1 tablespoon pepper**

Lightly flour brisket and brown both sides in a skillet. Transfer to a roasting pan. Brown onions and garlic in skillet. Place under and on top of brisket. Blend brown sugar, vinegar, ketchup, water, salt, and pepper. Pour over brisket. Cover and bake at 325 degrees for 2-3 hours.

YIELD: 15 SERVINGS

May double recipe using a larger brisket.

MAPLE GLAZED CORNED BEEF WITH CABBAGE

*The "corn" in "corned beef" refers to the "corns" or grains of coarse salt used to cure it.
The Oxford English dictionary dates the term "corned beef" to 1621.*

1 (6-8 pound) corned beef	**1 head cabbage, chopped**
8 teaspoons Dijon mustard	**2 tablespoons margarine**
6 tablespoons dark brown sugar	**Salt and pepper to taste**
1½ cups orange marmalade or apricot preserves	

Place corned beef in a large stockpot. Cover with cold water. Bring to boil. Reduce heat and simmer 3-4 hours or until tender. Transfer beef to a foil-lined shallow baking dish and reserve water. Blend mustard, brown sugar and marmalade. Pour glaze over meat. Bake at 400 degrees for 30 minutes.

Boil cabbage in reserved beef water for 15 minutes until tender. Drain and add margarine, tossing to coat. Add salt and pepper. Thinly slice corned beef against the grain. Surround with cooked cabbage.

YIELD: 10 TO 12 SERVINGS

TENDERLOIN ROAST WITH JEZEBEL SAUCE

JEZEBEL SAUCE
⅔ cup pineapple preserves
½ cup apple jelly

2 tablespoons prepared white horseradish
1 tablespoon grated ginger

JEZEBEL SAUCE

Cook pineapple preserves and apple jelly in a saucepan until melted and smooth. Stir in horseradish and ginger. Set aside.

TENDERLOIN
½ cup soy sauce
2 tablespoons brown sugar
2 green onions, chopped

2 tablespoons sherry
3 pound tenderloin roast

TENDERLOIN

Combine soy sauce, brown sugar, green onions, and sherry in a zip-top plastic bag or shallow dish. Add tenderloin and turn to coat. Refrigerate for at least 20 minutes or overnight.

Grill tenderloin or bake at 400 degrees for 15 minutes. Turn meat and baste with ½ cup Jezebel sauce. Grill or bake an additional 10 minutes. Remove from heat and let stand 10 minutes. Slice roast and pour the remaining Jezebel sauce over top.

FRIED GREEN TOMATOES

4 green tomatoes cut into ¼-inch rings
½ cup all-purpose flour
Salt and pepper
3 eggs

¼ cup water
1 cup cornmeal crumbs
1 tablespoon lemon pepper
Seasoned salt and cayenne pepper
Oil

Heat oil in a skillet to high heat. In a dish put flour seasoned with salt and pepper. In another dish beat eggs and with ¼ cup of water to make an egg wash. In a third dish combine cornmeal crumbs and lemon pepper. Dredge tomatoes through the flour, then the eggs, and then through the cornmeal mixture. Add a few slices to the skillet and fry on each side until browned — approximately 1-3 minutes. Drain on paper towels and season with seasoned salt and cayenne pepper to taste!

STEAK-LIKE SHOULDER ROAST

A glorious dish befitting the joy of the Sabbath! Pair with Shiraz,
Chianti, Cabernet Sauvignon, American Riesling, or Pinot Gris.

1 (10-12 pound) beef shoulder roast	2 tablespoons garlic powder
1 head garlic	2 tablespoons Hungarian paprika
2 tablespoons salt	1 (8 ounce) jar sweet and sour sauce
1 tablespoon pepper	

Rinse beef and cut deep slits all over. Insert garlic cloves into slits. Combine salt, pepper, garlic powder, and paprika. Rub mixture over entire roast. Place in a shallow roasting pan. Spread half sweet and sour sauce over top of roast. Bake at 425 degrees for 20 minutes. Reduce heat to 325 degrees and bake a total of 20 minutes per pound for medium rare, basting with remaining sweet and sour sauce.

To serve hot, cut into steak-like thickness. This roast is not served with any gravy.

To serve cold, slice very thin, deli-style.

YIELD: 10 TO 12 SERVINGS

SHORT RIBS AND BUTTER BEANS

Butter beans and lima beans are actually two different
varieties of lima beans. Butter beans are also known as Fordhook beans.

2 tablespoons mustard	1½ tablespoons soy sauce
1 (14 ounce) bottle ketchup	3 onions, sliced
½ cup packed brown sugar	2 pounds butter beans or
1 cup dark corn syrup	1 pound butter beans and
2 garlic cloves, minced	1 pound lima beans
2 teaspoons Worcestershire sauce	20 short ribs

Combine mustard, ketchup, brown sugar, corn syrup, garlic, Worcestershire sauce, and soy sauce. Place half onions in bottom of roasting pan. Scatter 1 pound beans over onions. Pour half sauce over beans. Place ribs on top. Spread remaining onions, 1 pound beans, and sauce on top. Cover and bake at 350 degrees for 1 hour, 30 minutes-2 hours or until meat is tender. If not tender, reduce heat to 325 degrees and bake until tender.

YIELD: 6 SERVINGS

Meats

SOUTHERN SPRING VEGETABLES AND VEAL RAGOÛT

*The term "ragoût" can refer to either a main dish stew or a
sauce for noodles or rice. Ragoûts are usually slow-cooked over low heat.*

3	pounds veal, cubed	1	pound asparagus, trimmed and cut into 1½-inch pieces
	Salt and pepper to taste		
1	tablespoon olive oil	2	leeks, mostly white parts, cut into ¼-inch rounds
3	cups chicken broth	2	cups frozen peas
8	plum tomatoes, quartered		
18	baby carrots		

Sprinkle veal with salt and pepper. Heat oil in a large skillet. Brown veal about 7-10 minutes. Add broth and tomatoes. Bring to boil. Reduce heat, cover and cook on medium-low for 20 minutes. Add carrots, asparagus, leeks, and peas. Cook at least 15 minutes or until tender. Serve over Curly Lemon Noodles in a soup bowl.

YIELD: 8 TO 10 SERVINGS

CURLY LEMON NOODLES

8 ounces curly wide egg noodles, cooked al dente	2 tablespoons chopped chives
2 tablespoons margarine, melted	2 teaspoons lemon zest
2 tablespoons chopped Italian flat-leaf parsley	1 teaspoon salt
	⅛ teaspoon pepper

Combine noodles, margarine, parsley, chives,
lemon zest, salt, and pepper. Mix well.

YIELD: 4 SERVINGS

FINGER LICKIN' SWEET AND SOUR SHORT RIBS

The secret to successful "sweet and sour" combinations is ingredients that work together to trigger the two parts in the mouth responsible for sensing sweet and sour sensations. The result should be a sweet taste and sour sensation in the mouth.

2	quarts sauerkraut	1	tablespoon granulated citric acid or sour salt
1	(15 ounce) can tomato sauce		
1	package non-sugar sweetener	1	(6 ounce) can tomato paste
1	pound brown sugar	1	(28 ounce) can chopped tomatoes
	Juice of 2 lemons	8-15	short ribs with bones

Combine sauerkraut, tomato sauce, sweetener, brown sugar, lemon juice, citric acid or sour salt, tomato paste, and tomatoes. Pour sauce in a roasting pan. Place ribs in sauce. Place pan over two stove burners. Bring to boil. Reduce heat and simmer about 4 hours until ribs are tender. Cool.

Transfer ribs from sauce to another pan. Cool sauce and skim off fat. Return ribs to sauce. Reheat and serve.

YIELD: 8 SERVINGS

This freezes well and is great for a crowd.

BLUE RIBBON VEAL CHOPS

The cut of meat known as the "chop" originated in 17th century Britain, when London chophouses started cooking individual portions of meat.

4	teaspoons vegetable oil	¼	teaspoon sugar
3	tablespoons soy sauce	¼	teaspoon pepper
3	tablespoons ketchup	1-2	garlic cloves, minced
1	tablespoon vinegar	2	veal chops, 1-inch thick

Blend oil, soy sauce, ketchup, vinegar, sugar, pepper, and garlic. Pour over chops and marinate at room temperature for 3 hours. Grill or broil about 10 minutes per side.

YIELD: 2 SERVINGS

Meats

SIMPLE VEAL SCALOPPINI

Scaloppini is a classic dish using a very thin protein.
It can be made with alternatives to veal, such as chicken, salmon and tofu.

½	cup all-purpose flour or cake meal	2	(15 ounce) cans *DonPepino* pizza sauce
¼	teaspoon pepper	1	tablespoon sugar
2	pounds veal cutlets	¼	teaspoon garlic powder
¼	cup vegetable oil	½	cup water
3	bell peppers, cut into strips		Salt to taste

Combine flour and pepper. Dredge cutlets in flour mixture. Heat oil in a skillet. Cook cutlet until browned on both sides. Drain on paper towels. Cook pepper, pizza sauce, sugar, garlic powder, and water in skillet. Return cutlets to the skillet. Bring to boil. Reduce heat, cover and simmer 10-15 minutes or until veal is cooked. Sprinkle with salt.

YIELD: 6 SERVINGS

VEAL BRISKET

Veal brisket is the boned veal breast. A moderately dry white wine,
like a Riesling, adds a little complexity to the finished dish.

2½-3	pound veal brisket	1	teaspoon dried rosemary
1	(1¼ ounce) package dry onion soup mix	1-2	teaspoons minced garlic
			Pepper to taste
½	cup dry white wine	6	red new potatoes
2	cups water	6	carrots, sliced into diagonal pieces
2	tablespoons tomato paste		
2	teaspoons paprika		

Place oven on broil. Broil veal on both sides until browned. Drain fat. Place in a roasting pan. Preheat oven to 325 degrees. Combine soup mix, wine, and water. Pour into pan. Spread tomato paste over veal. Sprinkle with paprika, rosemary, garlic, and pepper. Cover and bake for 1 hour, 30 minutes. Turn meat over and baste with pan juices. Bake an additional 30 minutes. Add potatoes and carrots. Bake 30-45 more minutes.

YIELD: 6 TO 8 SERVINGS

CHILI

One key to great chili is great spices. Store spices in a cool dry place.

2   pounds ground chuck
1   cup chopped onions
¼   cup chopped bell pepper
1   garlic clove, minced
2   (16 ounce) cans diced tomatoes, undrained
1   (16 ounce) can kidney beans, drained and rinsed
1   (15 ounce) can DonPepino pizza sauce

1   (4 ounce) can green chilies
1   jalapeño pepper, seeded and chopped
1   package spicy chili seasoning mix
1   teaspoon dried oregano
2   teaspoons ground cumin
½   teaspoon dried basil
1½ teaspoons salt
¼   teaspoon pepper

Cook meat, onion, pepper, and garlic in a 4-quart Dutch oven until meat is browned. Drain drippings. Add tomatoes with juice, kidney beans, pizza sauce, chilies, jalapeño pepper, chili seasoning, oregano, cumin, basil, salt, and pepper. Cook over medium heat for 10 minutes. Reduce heat, cover and simmer for 1 hour.

YIELD: 6 TO 8 SERVINGS

SOUTHERN SMOTHERED BURGERS

3	medium-large yellow onions, sliced	1	teaspoon garlic powder
2	eggs, beaten	3	pounds ground beef
2	teaspoons seasoned salt	⅓	cup plain bread crumbs
1	teaspoon pepper	¾	cup matzo meal
		1-1½	cans beef broth

Preheat oven to 400 degrees. Heat a greased 12-inch skillet over medium-high heat. Sauté onions until browned. Beat eggs, seasoned salt, pepper, and garlic powder in a bowl. Add meat and bread crumbs. Mix well. Shape meat mixture into patties. Place matzo meal on a plate. Coat patties on all sides with meal. Brown patties in a greased sauté pan until browned and almost cooked through. Place patties in a greased 13 x 9 x 2-inch baking dish.

Add onions to skillet with meat drippings and mix well. Spread onions under and over patties. Pour broth over burgers. Bake, uncovered, at 400 degrees for 40-45 minutes. Longer baking time enhances the flavors of the onions, gravy and burgers.

YIELD: 6 TO 8 SERVINGS

STANDING RIB-EYE ROAST

*Generally speaking, a roast is a cut of beef that is
at least 2-inches thick. A thinner cut is usually called a steak.*

2	tablespoons onion powder	¾	cup water
2	tablespoons garlic powder	2	tablespoons olive oil
1	teaspoon seasoned salt	1	tablespoon soy sauce
1	teaspoon pepper		Whole garlic cloves
1	tablespoon paprika	6	pound rib-eye roast with or without bones
1	tablespoon dried parsley		

Blend onion powder, garlic powder, seasoned salt, pepper, paprika, parsley, and water until smooth. Add oil and soy sauce. Place meat in a baking dish. Pierce holes in meat. Press garlic into holes. Pour three-fourths marinade over meat. Pierce a few more holes in meat and pour on remaining marinade. Add 1½-2 cups water to bottom of baking dish. Refrigerate overnight. Bake at 350 degrees 20 minutes per pound.

YIELD: 8 TO 10 SERVINGS

TENNESSEE BEEF RIBS

Memphis, Barbeque, Beef. Ribs. 'Nuff said.

2   packages beef ribs, cut apart with
    fat removed from back of bone
2   bottles hickory flavored barbeque
    sauce

2   bottles honey smoke flavored
    barbeque sauce
¼   cup liquid smoke
¾   cup honey
2   cups semi-sweet wine

Combine barbeque sauces, liquid smoke, honey, and wine. Place ribs in marinade and mix
well. Marinate for a few hours. Remove ribs from marinade and place in a roasting pan, reserving
marinade. Cover with foil. Bake at 350 degrees for 2 hours. Remove from oven and drain
drippings. Pour on reserved marinade. Return to oven and bake uncovered for 1 hour,
30 minutes-2 hours until browned and tender.

YIELD: 10 SERVINGS

CHICKEN FRIED STEAK AND GRAVY

Have nice bread on hand to sop up the extra gravy!

STEAK
3	tablespoons vegetable oil	⅓	cup all-purpose flour
3	tablespoons margarine	1	egg
¾	teaspoon salt	¾	cup bread crumbs
¾	teaspoon pepper	6	(4 ounce) cubed steaks (boneless and tenderized)

STEAK

Heat oil and margarine in a large skillet. Combine salt, pepper and flour in one bowl. Beat egg in a second bowl. Place bread crumbs in a third bowl. Dredge steaks in flour mixture and then egg. Press steak into bread crumbs. Pan fry steaks in hot skillet until golden brown on both sides. Transfer to a dish to keep warm.

GRAVY
¼	cup all-purpose flour	¼	cup chicken broth
1	cup soymilk		Salt and pepper to taste

GRAVY

Whisk in flour, soymilk and broth to deglaze skillet until thickened into a gravy. Add salt and pepper. Pour gravy over steaks.

YIELD: 6 SERVINGS

This Southern dish is served with mashed potatoes! Chicken Fried Steak is an old Southern favorite. It is made from a thin cut of steak that has been tenerized by pounding. It was originally developed to create an inexpensive meat dish. It is traditionally served with mashed potatoes to make good use of that gravy.

YOUR MAMA'S MASHED POTATOES

2 pounds potatoes, peeled and quartered	1 cup soymilk
Salt and freshly ground black pepper	1 stick margarine

Put potatoes in a large pot and cover with cold water. Add 1 tablespoon of salt and bring to a boil. Reduce the heat and simmer, uncovered, until the potatoes are tender, about 30 minutes. Melt margarine. Add soymilk to margarine and keep warm until potatoes are ready. Drain potatoes and then put back into the pot while they are still hot. Pour soymilk and margarine into pot with potatoes and mash! Season with salt and pepper to taste!

SPAGHETTI AND MEAT SAUCE

"Spaghetti" can be literally translated as "little strings."
The average American eats about 20 pounds of pasta a year.

	Extra virgin olive oil
4	garlic cloves, minced
2	pounds ground beef
1	tablespoon dried basil
1	teaspoon kosher salt
1	teaspoon pepper

1	teaspoon dried oregano
2	(12 ounce) cans tomato paste
3	cans water
1	pound spaghetti, cooked al dente

Add oil to a large stockpot. Sauté garlic for 1 minute to release flavors. Cook beef until brown. Add basil, salt, pepper, and oregano. Add tomato paste and water. Do not want sauce too watery or too thick. Simmer uncovered for at least 1 hour. Serve sauce over hot pasta.

YIELD: 4 TO 6 SERVINGS

ROCK 'N REUBEN DELI ROLL

*A tried-and-true hit with the young and the not-so-young! Highly addictive—
this treat is a worthy splurge for even the most conscientious weight watchers.*

1	pound shredded corned beef	½	teaspoon pepper
½	(32 ounce) jar sauerkraut, drained	¼	cup brown mustard
½	cup mayonnaise	2	puff pastry sheets
2	large onions, chopped	1	egg, beaten
¼	teaspoon minced garlic	1	tablespoon water
¼	teaspoon paprika		Sesame seeds (optional)

Combine corned beef, sauerkraut, and mayonnaise. Sauté onions with garlic, paprika, pepper, and mustard. Add to corned beef mixture. Spread half mixture over each pastry sheet. Roll sheets into a log. Blend egg and water. Brush rolls lightly with the egg wash. Sprinkle with sesame seeds. Cut 3 diagonal slits across each roll. Bake at 350 degrees for 30-45 minutes or until brown and flaky.

YIELD: 8 TO 10 SERVINGS

SPICY SKILLET BEEF CRUMBLE

*Ground beef is the most popular cut of beef sold in the United States.
It accounts for 40 to 45 percent of all beef sold. Beef is the No.1 source of
protein, Vitamin B12 and zinc and the No.3 food source of iron.*

1	tablespoon margarine	1	tablespoon chopped parsley
1	onion, chopped	1	teaspoon Dijon mustard
2	garlic cloves, minced	1	teaspoon dried oregano
1	cup sliced mushrooms	1	teaspoon Worcestershire sauce
2	pounds ground beef	½	teaspoon salt
1	(15 ounce) can **Don Pepino** pizza sauce		Hot sauce to taste

Melt margarine in a large skillet. Sauté onion and garlic until tender. Add mushrooms and sauté until slightly browned. Add beef and cook until browned. Stir in pizza sauce, parsley, mustard, oregano, Worcestershire sauce, salt, and hot sauce. Cover and simmer for 10-15 minutes. Serve over hot rice or noodles.

YIELD: 6 SERVINGS

This is a great weeknight meal served over hot rice or noodles. The whole family will love it!

THE SOUTH'S SCRUMPTIOUS MEATLOAF

TOPPING

½ cup ketchup

2 tablespoons packed
   brown sugar

2 teaspoons cider vinegar

TOPPING

Blend ketchup, brown sugar and vinegar.

MEATLOAF

2 tablespoons margarine

1 medium onion, finely diced

2 cups fresh bread crumbs
   (5-6 slices ground white bread)

¼ cup soymilk

2 pounds ground beef

2 eggs

2 tablespoons white horseradish
   sauce

2 teaspoons kosher salt

¼ teaspoon pepper

1 teaspoon dry mustard

¼ cup ketchup

MEATLOAF

Preheat oven to 350 degrees. Melt margarine in a skillet. Sauté onion until tender and translucent. Set aside to cool. Soak bread crumbs in soymilk. Combine onion, bread crumb mixture, beef, eggs, horseradish, salt, pepper, mustard, and ketchup. Mix well with hands. Shape mixture into a 10 x 5-inch loaf. Press firmly into a 13 x 9 x 2-inch baking dish. Spread topping over loaf. Bake on middle rack at 350 degrees for 45 minutes-1 hour. Let rest 10 minutes before serving.

YIELD: 6 TO 8 SERVINGS

SPICY SZECHUAN BEEF

MARINADE
¼ cup soy sauce

1 tablespoon vinegar

1 tablespoon sugar

1 teaspoon finely chopped ginger

MARINADE

Blend soy sauce, vinegar, sugar, and ginger.

BEEF
1 pound boneless beef, cut into thin strips

¼ cup vegetable oil, divided

1½ cups julienne cut carrots

1 cup julienne cut celery

½ cup julienne cut hot green chili peppers

8 dried hot red chili peppers

½ teaspoon peppercorns

BEEF

Add beef strips into marinade. Marinate for 30 minutes. Heat 2 tablespoons oil in a wok. Stir-fry carrot, celery, and chili peppers for 1-3 minutes. Transfer vegetables to a platter. Add remaining 2 tablespoons oil to the wok. Add dried chili peppers and cook until dark brown. Add beef and stir-fry until all liquid evaporates. Reduce heat, return cooked vegetables to wok and add peppercorns. Mix well and serve hot.

YIELD: 4 SERVINGS

VEAL STEW

2-2½ pounds veal stew meat

Salt and pepper to taste

3 tablespoons all-purpose flour

3 tablespoons vegetable oil

2 medium onions, diced

3 carrots, sliced

1 stalk celery, chopped

3 garlic cloves, minced

1 (8 ounce) can stewed tomatoes, undrained

1 cup white wine

1 (15 ounce) can *Don Pepino* pizza sauce

2-3 bay leaves

Pinch of dried thyme

Sprinkle veal with salt and pepper. Dust with flour. Heat oil in a skillet over medium heat. Cook veal for 10 minutes until browned. Add onion, carrot, celery, and garlic. Cook for 3-5 minutes. Pour in tomatoes with juice, wine, pizza sauce, bay leaves, and thyme. Bring to boil. Reduce heat, cover and simmer for 1 hour-1 hour, 30 minutes.

YIELD: 6 SERVINGS

MESS OF UNSTUFFED CABBAGE

A deconstructed version of the Old Country peasant favorite.

½ cup water
2 tablespoons vegetable oil, divided
½ teaspoon kosher salt
1 cup rice, uncooked
2 onions, halved and sliced
2 pounds ground beef
Salt and pepper to taste

1 tablespoon garlic powder
1 (8 ounce) can whole cranberry sauce
1 (12 ounce) bottle chili sauce
3 tablespoons lemon juice
¼ cup packed dark brown sugar
1 package angel hair cabbage

Preheat oven to 350 degrees. Bring water to boil in a saucepan. Add 1 tablespoon oil and salt. Add rice, reduce heat, cover and simmer. When rice is level with water, place covered pan in the oven. Bake at 350 degrees for 15-20 minutes until water is absorbed. Rice will be par-cooked and texture slightly hard. Set aside.

Brown onion in 1 tablespoon oil in large pot. Add beef, salt, pepper, and garlic powder. Cook and stir 15 minutes until beef is browned. Remove from heat. Add rice to meat mixture and mix well.

Combine cranberry sauce, chili sauce, lemon juice, and brown sugar in a bowl. Mix well. Stir in cabbage. To assemble, spread half meat/rice mixture into bottom of a 13 x 9 x 2-inch baking dish. Top with half of the cabbage sauce mixture. Repeat both layers. Cover and bake at 350 degrees for 1 hour. Uncover and bake an additional 20 minutes.

SWEET AND SOUR MEATBALLS

MEAT MIXTURE:
2 pounds ground beef
⅔ cup matzo meal
½ cup water
2 eggs, slightly beaten

½ cup minced onion
1 teaspoon salt
¼ teaspoon pepper

SAUCE:
1 large onion, finely chopped in food processor
½ cup lemon juice
1 cup sugar

1 (15 ounce) can *DonPepino* pizza sauce
½ cup water

Combine beef, matzo meal, water, eggs, ½ cup onion, salt, and pepper. Wet hands and then shape into small meatballs. In large pot combine 1 large onion from processor, lemon juice, sugar, pizza sauce, and water. Add meatballs. Bring to a boil, reduce heat, and simmer for about 1 hour. Serves 6 or more if main dish or many more as an appetizer. Can be frozen!

Poultry

To our favorite Chef, Laurie Smith
She nourishes our hearts and souls with love and makes the best food in the world.
Sheldon, Garrett and Sonny

Sue Ann Lipsey, whose "Real Fried Chicken" graces the cover of this book, is well known in Memphis as a Southern gal who is always happy to share a recipe. Originally from Blytheville, Arkansas, Sue Ann has been cooking as long as she can remember. "I love cooking magazines and always try to make their recipes kosher." Sue Ann's fried chicken recipe is one of many she adapted herself, much to the delight of her family and friends. "My advice to any cook is to just try a new recipe because entertaining is very rewarding." As her recipes firmly attest, creatively reinventing Southern classics is an art, fondly shared with others.

CHICKEN FRICASSEE

Be sure to have plenty of bread because your guests will want to sop up every last drop! Makes a great appetizer-serve as a first course in small bowls.

1	tablespoon margarine	1	egg
½	chicken fryer, cut into small pieces	2	tablespoons finely diced onion
3	large onions, diced	2	tablespoons matzo meal
3	tablespoons paprika		Salt and pepper to taste
1	pound ground beef		

Melt margarine in a large stockpot. Add chicken, onion and paprika. Increase heat to high and cook until onion and chicken are well browned. Fill pot halfway with water. Bring to boil. Reduce heat.

Combine beef, egg, onion, meal, salt, and pepper in a bowl. Shape mixture into 1 to 2-inch meatballs. Bring chicken pot to boil. Reduce heat and add meatballs. Cover and simmer for 1½-2 hours.

YIELD: 6 SERVINGS

ORANGE ALMOND CHICKEN

This dish satisfies the palate with the robust combination of citrus and nuts.

4-6	boneless, skinless chicken breast halves		All-purpose flour, salt, pepper, and garlic powder to taste
1½	cups orange juice	3-4	tablespoons vegetable oil
6	garlic cloves, crushed	1	cup chicken broth
3	tablespoons chopped parsley	½	cup sliced almonds

Marinate chicken in orange juice, garlic and parsley for at least 4 hours. Discard all but ¼ cup marinade. Combine flour, salt, pepper, and garlic powder. Dredge chicken in flour mixture. Cook in oil until lightly browned. Place chicken in a baking dish. Add broth and reserved marinade to skillet. Cook for 10 minutes. Add almonds and cook for few minutes. Pour sauce over chicken. Cover and bake at 325 degrees for 30 minutes. Uncover and bake an additional 15 minutes.

YIELD: 4 TO 6 SERVINGS

BASIL MARINATED GRILLED CHICKEN

Fresh basil grows abundantly in the South!
We find many ways to incorporate it into our cooking!

2 pounds boneless, skinless chicken breast halves	2 teaspoons minced garlic
	Kosher salt and pepper to taste
1 cup basil leaves	½ cup olive oil

Pound chicken to ¼- to ½-inch thickness. Combine basil, garlic, salt, and pepper in a food processor. Process until combined. Slowly add oil and process until smooth. Pour marinade into a zip-top plastic bag. Add chicken and marinate a few hours or overnight.

Remove chicken from marinade. Grill over medium-high heat for 7-10 minutes per side.

YIELD: 6 TO 8 SERVINGS

THAI-SPICED CILANTRO CHICKEN

Cilantro is part of the coriander plant. It is used with salads,
fish, chicken, and many other dishes lending its lively and pungent flavor.
It may be stored up to a week in a plastic bag in the refrigerator. Both the
leaves and tender stems may be used in fresh or cooked dishes.

4 boneless, skinless chicken breast halves	¼ cup chopped cilantro
	Zest of 1 lime
2 garlic cloves	3 tablespoons lime juice
1 green chili pepper	2 tablespoons light soy sauce
¾ inch ginger piece	¾ cup cream of coconut

Using a sharp knife, cut slits into chicken. Place in a dish. Combine garlic, chili pepper, ginger, cilantro, lime zest, lime juice, soy sauce, and coconut cream in a food processor. Process until smooth. Spread purée over chicken. Cover and marinate at least 1 hour or overnight.

Drain marinade from chicken and place on a baking sheet or broiling pan. Broil about 15-20 minutes, turning once until evenly cooked. Pour marinade into saucepan. Bring to boil. Reduce heat and simmer for several minutes. Pour sauce over chicken.

YIELD: 4 SERVINGS

CHICKEN BREASTS WITH LEMONS, ARTICHOKES AND MUSHROOMS

Artichokes are an edible thistle that was prized by ancient Romans as a food of the nobility. Serve this in a casserole dish— the lemony sauce with the mushrooms and artichokes tastes great!

⅓ cup vegetable oil

8 boneless, skinless chicken breast halves, pounded to ½-inch thickness

1 tablespoon margarine

2 garlic cloves, minced

½ pound sliced mushrooms

½ lemon, thinly sliced

1 tablespoon all-purpose flour

1 teaspoon salt

½ teaspoon pepper

½ teaspoon dried oregano

¾ cup white wine

1 (14 ounce) can artichokes, drained and quartered

Heat oil in a large skillet. Cook chicken on each side until tender and lightly browned. Transfer chicken to a plate. Melt margarine in skillet. Add garlic, mushrooms and lemon slices. Cook about 3 minutes until tender. Stir in flour, salt, pepper, and oregano until well combined. Pour in wine. Bring to boil, stirring until sauce thickens. Add artichokes and return chicken to skillet. Simmer 2 minutes or heated through.

YIELD: 8 SERVINGS

LEMONY, LEMONY RICE

Zest of 1 lemon

Juice of 2 lemons (⅓ cup)

1⅓ cups rice

2⅓ cups chicken broth

Combine lemon zest, juice, rice, and broth. Bring to a boil.
Reduce heat to low and simmer. Cover until rice is tender
and liquid is absorbed, about 20 minutes.

SWEET AND SOUR CHICKEN

Contrast is the key! Sweet and sour flavors combine with crunchy and moist textures to make this Chinese classic! Turkey breast or veal may substitute for chicken.

BATTER

4	eggs	1	teaspoon salt
1½	cups all-purpose flour	16	tablespoons water

BATTER

Whisk together eggs, flour, salt, and water until smooth.

CHICKEN

3	pounds chicken breast halves	1	red bell pepper, chopped
1	green bell pepper, chopped	1	onion, chopped

CHICKEN

Dip cutlets into batter. Pan fry in oil until lightly browned on both sides. Transfer to a 13 x 9 x 2-inch baking dish. Sauté pepper and onion until tender. Spoon vegetables over chicken. Pour sauce over chicken. Bake, uncovered, at 350 degrees for 30 minutes.

SAUCE

½	cup sugar	¾	cup soy sauce
1½	cups distilled vinegar	5	tablespoons cornstarch
¾	cup ketchup		

SAUCE

Combine sugar, vinegar, ketchup, soy sauce, and cornstarch in a saucepan. Bring to boil and whisk until sauce thickens. Keep warm.

YIELD: 8 TO 10 SERVINGS

Sweet and Sour Chicken is ideal for a big family dinner when you have a lot of dishes to prepare. You can break this one down into stages. You can sauté your vegetables one day then pan fry the chicken breasts the next day. The day of the dinner put it together and top with sauce and keep warm. Or you can make it ahead and freeze without the sauce. Defrost, reheat and pour sauce over to serve!

Poultry

ITALIAN STYLE CHICKEN SCHNITZEL WITH ITALIAN SPINACH

- 3 tablespoons vegetable oil
- 5 tablespoons margarine
- 2 cups plain bread crumbs, reserve ⅓ cup
- ⅔ cup all-purpose flour
- 1 tablespoon garlic powder
- 1 tablespoon paprika
- 1 teaspoon dried oregano
- 1 teaspoon dried basil
- 1 teaspoon salt
- 1 teaspoon pepper
- 3 eggs, divided
- 2 pounds chicken breast halves, pounded to ½-inch thickness
- 2 (10 ounce) packages fresh spinach

Heat margarine and oil in a skillet over medium high heat. Combine bread crumbs, flour, garlic powder, paprika, oregano, basil, salt, and pepper in a dish. Beat one egg. Dip chicken into egg and dredge in bread crumb mixture. Fry chicken until browned and cooked on both sides. Transfer chicken to a platter and keep warm.

Stir-fry spinach in hot skillet. When almost cooked, add one beaten egg and one whole egg. Cook and stir egg into spinach. Sprinkle with reserved bread crumbs. Add salt and pepper. Serve chicken with spinach.

YIELD: 6 TO 8 SERVINGS

Add garlic to spinach to increase flavor. Serve with **DonPepino** *pizza sauce on top or on side of chicken.*

HARVEST CHICKEN

- 1 onion, sliced
- 3 pounds chicken, cut up
  Season to taste
- 1 pound butternut squash, peeled and cut up
- ½ teaspoon nutmeg
- 1 cup dried prunes
- ½ cup orange juice

Place onion in bottom of pan. Put chicken in pan and season. Add squash; season with nutmeg. Add prunes. Pour orange juice over all and cover well. Bake at 350 degrees for 1-1½ hours. Freezes well.

CHINESE SESAME CHICKEN

This is one you will make over and over!

2	eggs	½	teaspoon salt
2	tablespoons soy sauce	½	teaspoon pepper
2	tablespoons water	1	pound boneless chicken breast halves
1	cup bread crumbs	½	cup apricot preserves
½	cup sesame seeds	2	tablespoons soy sauce
1	teaspoon paprika	1	garlic clove
½	teaspoon garlic powder		Chili sauce

Whisk together eggs, soy sauce and water. Combine bread crumbs, sesame seeds, paprika, garlic powder, salt, and pepper. Dip chicken into egg mixture. Dredge in bread crumb mixture. Cook in a sauté pan until done. Blend apricot preserves, soy sauce, garlic, and chili sauce. Pour sauce over chicken before serving.

YIELD: 6 TO 8 SERVINGS

LEMON CHICKEN

Rosemary is a member of the mint family and has been used to cure ailments of the nervous system. Its silver-green needle—shaped leaves are highly aromatic and combine perfectly with lemon.

1	tablespoon olive oil		Zest of 1 lemon
2	garlic cloves, minced	4	boneless, skinless chicken breast halves
1	tablespoon chopped rosemary	1	egg white, slightly beaten
¾	cup dry bread crumbs		Juice of 1 lemon
	Salt and pepper to taste		Lemon wedges for garnish

Heat oil in a skillet. Sauté garlic and rosemary for 30 seconds. Stir in bread crumbs, salt, pepper, and lemon zest. Dip chicken into egg white. Dredge in bread crumb mixture. Place in a greased baking dish. Pour lemon juice over chicken. Bake at 400 degrees at least 30 minutes. Serve with lemon wedges.

YIELD: 4 SERVINGS

SOUTHERN STYLE SESAME CHICKEN STRIPS

These chicken strips are baked and freeze well. They are great for a crowd and children love them!

- 1 cup mayonnaise
- 1 teaspoon dry mustard
- 1 tablespoon minced onion
- 2 pounds boneless, skinless chicken breast halves, cut into strips
- 2 cups seasoned bread crumbs
- ½ cup sesame seeds

Preheat oven to 375 degrees. Combine mayonnaise, mustard, and onion. In a separate bowl combine bread crumbs and sesame seeds. Spread mayonnaise over chicken. Roll in bread crumb mixture. Place in a greased 13 x 9 x 2-inch baking dish. Bake at 375 degrees for 30-45 minutes. May turn chicken halfway through baking.

YIELD: 8 TO 10 SERVINGS

CHICKEN STRIP SAUCE

½ cup mayonnaise

1 tablespoon Dijon mustard

2 tablespoons maple syrup

Mix mayonnaise, maple syrup, and mustard. Serve on the side.

APPLE DIJON SKILLET CHICKEN

- 4 boneless, skinless chicken breast halves
- 1 tablespoon olive oil
- 2 apples, cored and each cut into 6 rings
- 1 small onion, sliced
- ¾ cup chicken broth
- 2 tablespoons maple syrup
- 1 tablespoon coarse Dijon mustard
- ¼ teaspoon salt
- ⅓ cup soymilk
- 1 teaspoon cornstarch

In 12-inch skillet, heat oil over medium high heat until hot. Add breasts and cook 6-7 minutes on each side until it is cooked throughout. Transfer breasts to platter and keep warm. In that same skillet, add apples and onion and sauté until browned. Add chicken stock, maple syrup, coarse Dijon mustard, and salt. Cook until sauce is reduced. Combine soymilk and cornstarch and stir into apple mixture to thicken into a sauce. Pour over chicken and serve!

PECAN CHICKEN BREASTS

*Pecans are a member of the hickory family
and are widely grown in the temperate climates of the South.*

*Store whole pecans in the shell tightly wrapped in a cool dry place for up to six months.
Refrigerate shelled pecans in an airtight container for up to 3 months or freeze up to 6 months.*

1 stick margarine, divided	1 tablespoon vegetable oil
2 tablespoons Dijon mustard	½ teaspoon salt
1½ cups finely chopped pecans	¼ teaspoon pepper
8 boneless skinless chicken breast halves, pounded to ¼-inch thickness	

Melt 6 tablespoons margarine in a small saucepan. Whisk in mustard until blended. Scrape into a shallow dish. Place pecan into another shallow dish. Dip chicken into mustard mixture. Dredge in pecans until well coated. Heat remaining 2 tablespoons margarine and oil in a skillet over medium heat. Add chicken. Sprinkle with salt and pepper. Cook for 3 minutes per side until lightly browned and tender.

YIELD: 8 SERVINGS

QUICK THAI CHICKEN CURRY

*Cool coconut milk balances the fiery spices, making a mouthful of yummy contrast.
This is a quick and easy dish to make for a satisfying and different weeknight meal.*

1 (14 ounce) can stewed tomatoes	1 pound boneless skinless chicken breast halves, cut into ¾-inch cubes
2 teaspoons curry powder or more to taste	Salt and pepper to taste
½ teaspoon lime zest	¾ cup coconut milk
1 teaspoon sugar	3 tablespoons thinly sliced basil
½ teaspoon minced jalapeño pepper	

Combine tomatoes, curry, lime zest, sugar, and jalapeño pepper in a skillet. Cook and stir over medium heat. Sprinkle chicken with salt and pepper. Add chicken, coconut milk and basil to skillet. Cook 8 minutes until chicken is done.

YIELD: 6 SERVINGS

SPRING VEGETABLE ASIAN CHICKEN

Once you make this dish, it will become a regular in your meal planning.

3   tablespoons vegetable oil
1   pound boneless skinless chicken breast halves, cubed
2   (3 ounce) packages chicken flavored Ramen noodles
1   medium zucchini, sliced
1   medium yellow squash, sliced

2   stalks celery, thinly sliced on bias
3   garlic cloves, minced
1   cup water
⅓   cup bottled sweet and sour sauce
⅓   cup cashews
1   (11 ounce) can Mandarin oranges, drained

Heat oil in a large skillet or wok over medium heat. Stir fry chicken until done. Transfer to a platter. Break up Ramen noodles. Add noodles, zucchini, squash, celery, garlic, and water. Bring to boil. Reduce heat, cover and simmer 3-5 minutes or until noodles and vegetables are tender. May need more water. Return chicken and add noodle seasoning packet, sweet and sour sauce, and cashews. Heat thoroughly. Just before serving add oranges.

YIELD: 6 SERVINGS

CHICKEN AND RICE

Everybody loves this perfectly put together classic!

1   cup rice, uncooked
½   teaspoon celery seeds
½   teaspoon dried oregano
½   teaspoon salt
½   teaspoon dried parsley

1   (15 ounce) can chicken broth
1   can water
2   cut up chickens
    Salt and pepper to taste
    Vegetable oil

Spread rice in bottom of a greased 2-quart casserole dish. Layer in order: celery seed, oregano, salt, parsley, broth, and water. Sprinkle chicken with salt and pepper. Dip in oil. Place in casserole dish. Cover and bake at 350 degrees for 2 hours.

YIELD: 8 SERVINGS

CHICKEN WITH NEVER FAIL DUMPLINGS

Genuine stick-to-your-ribs Cotton Country goodness!

DUMPLING

- 2 cups sifted all-purpose flour
- 1 teaspoon salt
- 4 teaspoons baking powder
- 2 tablespoons vegetable shortening
- ¾ cup plus 2 tablespoons water

DUMPLINGS

Combine flour, salt, baking powder, and shortening with your hands until a soft dough forms. Slowly add water until a thick batter forms. Roll out batter with flour to ¼- to ⅓-inch thickness. Cut into 2½-inch long x ½-inch wide strips.

CHICKEN

- 1 (5-6 pound) chicken, skinned and cut into pieces
- 1 parsnip, peeled, left whole
- 3 large carrots, cut into 3 pieces
- 5 stalks celery with tops, chopped
- 1 very large onion, quartered
- 1½ teaspoons salt
- ⅓ teaspoon white pepper
- ½ cup chicken broth
- 16 cups water

CHICKEN

Combine chicken, parsnip, carrot, celery, onion, salt, pepper, broth, and water in a large stockpot. Bring to boil. Reduce heat and simmer until chicken is very tender. Remove from heat and cool. Strain broth into a separate bowl. Cut or pull apart chicken and place in another bowl. Add 8 cups broth back to pot. Bring to boil. Add dumplings and chicken. Simmer for 20 minutes or until dumplings are done.

YIELD: 8 SERVINGS

Dumplings have been around for many years. Different cultures have their own versions of the tasty doughy treats made of flour, shortening, milk, and water or stock. In the South we like our dumplings with chicken. This dish is meant to be thick, warm, and comforting. You may want to double the dumpling recipe so that there will be enough dumplings for each bite of chicken. Chicken with Never Fail Dumplings is the definition of Southern comfort food!

REAL FRIED CHICKEN

*True Southerners make enough for leftovers. Nothing beats cold
fried chicken for lunch the day after. Do not skip the salt! Salt is an especially important
ingredient to the authentic taste of this signature dish of Dixie!*

MARINADE

1 quart water	1½ teaspoons white pepper
2 tablespoons salt	1 tablespoon soy sauce
2 teaspoons cayenne pepper	2 teaspoons Worcestershire sauce
2 teaspoons garlic powder	

MARINADE

Whisk together water, salt, cayenne, garlic powder, white pepper, soy sauce, and Worcestershire sauce in a large bowl.

CHICKEN

4 cut up chickens	3 cups all-purpose flour
12 cups vegetable oil	1 tablespoon salt
Self-rising flour	1 teaspoon garlic powder
2 eggs, beaten	1 teaspoon cayenne pepper
2 tablespoons water	1 teaspoon white pepper

CHICKEN

Add chicken pieces to marinade. Toss to coat. Cover and refrigerate for 24 hours.

Heat oil in a deep fryer to 360-375 degrees. Drain marinade from chicken on paper towels and pat dry. Sprinkle chicken on both sides with self-rising flour. Blend eggs and water. Combine all-purpose flour, salt, garlic powder, cayenne, and white pepper. Dip chicken in egg wash. Dredge in flour mixture. Place chicken on a large baking sheet. Let stand for 10 minutes. Fry chicken in hot oil turning a few times for 20-25 minutes or until golden browned. Drain on a rack over paper towels.

YIELD: 6 TO 8 SERVINGS

OVEN FRIED CHICKEN DRUMSTICKS

Down home Southern comfort!

½	cup all-purpose flour	2	teaspoons paprika
1	cup cornflake crumbs	¼	teaspoon pepper
1	cup bread crumbs	4	pounds chicken drumsticks (18 legs)
2	tablespoons dried parsley		
1½	teaspoons garlic powder	2	eggs, slightly beaten
1	teaspoon salt	3	tablespoons margarine

Preheat oven to 400 degrees. Combine flour, cornflake crumbs, bread crumbs, parsley, garlic powder, salt, paprika, and pepper. Dip drumsticks into egg. Roll in bread crumb mixture. Arrange drumsticks in a greased 13 x 9 x 2-inch baking dish. Drizzle margarine over chicken. Bake at 400 degrees for 1 hour.

YIELD: 4 TO 6 SERVINGS

APRICOT CHICKEN

The luscious apricot originated in China but Spanish explorers brought it to California, which grows about 95% of the United States crop. Apricot preserves are an excellent condiment for children.

2	tablespoons extra virgin olive oil	2	tablespoons cider or white wine vinegar
2	pounds boneless, skinless chicken breast halves, cut in half across on an angle	12	dried pitted apricots, chopped
	Salt and pepper to taste	2	cups chicken broth
		1	cup apricot spread or preserves
1	large onion, chopped	3	tablespoons chopped flat leaf parsley

Heat a large skillet over medium high heat. Add oil and chicken. Sprinkle with salt and pepper. Cook a few minutes until lightly browned. Add onion and cook 5 minutes. Pour in vinegar. Cook until liquid evaporates. Add apricots and broth. Bring to boil. Stir in preserves. Cover, reduce heat and simmer for 10-15 minutes. Top with parsley.

YIELD: 6 TO 8 SERVINGS

LITTLE RED CHICKEN

Take these leftovers and add soup broth and you have an incredible soup!

8	ounces sliced mushrooms	½	teaspoon dried oregano
½	cup sliced onions	¼	teaspoon cayenne pepper
½	cup chopped bell pepper	1	tablespoon Worcestershire sauce
1	garlic clove, chopped	1	(15 ounce) can *DonPepino* pizza sauce
3	pounds cubed chicken		
2	teaspoons chicken or beef bouillon granules	2	tablespoons brown sugar
		1	teaspoon dry mustard
½	cup water	1	teaspoon salt
1	bay leaf	¼	teaspoon pepper
1	tablespoon dried parsley	¼	teaspoon vinegar

Sauté mushrooms, onion, pepper, and garlic in a skillet. Place half vegetables on bottom of 13 x 9 x 2-inch baking dish. Spread chicken over top. Spoon remaining vegetables over chicken. Dissolve bouillon in water. Whisk together soup broth, bay leaf, parsley, oregano, cayenne, Worcestershire sauce, pizza sauce, brown sugar, mustard, salt, pepper, and vinegar. Pour sauce over vegetables. Bake at 350 degrees for 1-1½ hours.

YIELD: 8 TO 10 SERVINGS

TOMATO FENNEL CHICKEN

We love assembling-and-baking-it-the-next-day recipes!

2	(3 pound) whole chickens, cut up	2	onions, thinly sliced
6	garlic cloves, crushed	1	(28 ounce) can plum tomatoes, drained or 8 plum tomatoes, quartered
¼	cup olive oil		
½	cup lemon juice	¼	cup chopped parsley
	Salt and pepper to taste		
4	fennel bulbs, cut into eighths, reserve fronds for garnish		

Combine chicken, garlic, oil, lemon juice, salt, pepper, fennel, onion, tomatoes, and parsley. Mix well. Marinate for several hours or overnight. Place chicken in a baking dish. Roast at 400 degrees for 45 minutes or until juices run clear.

YIELD: 10 TO 12 SERVINGS

CHICKEN PANDORA

*Mythical like its namesake! This recipe has a lot of
ingredients and takes time to make, but it is worth it! Freezes great!*

½	cup red wine vinegar	2	pounds boneless skinless chicken breast halves, cut into bite size pieces
½	cup plus 1 tablespoon olive oil		
½	cup chopped oregano or ⅛ cup dried	¾	cup packed brown sugar
¼	cup chopped parsley	1	cup dry red wine
1	head garlic, peeled and puréed	8	shallots, chopped
	Kosher salt and pepper to taste	1	tablespoon margarine
3	bay leaves	1	cup sun-dried tomatoes
1	cup ripe black olives, halved	2	(16 ounce) cans artichokes hearts, drained and quartered
			Hot cooked rice or couscous

Combine vinegar, ½ cup oil, oregano, parsley, garlic, salt, pepper, bay leaves, and olive in a greased 13 x 9 x 2-inch baking dish. Add chicken and toss to coat. Cover and refrigerate overnight.

Sprinkle chicken with brown sugar and wine. Cover and bake at 350 degrees for 1 hour. Sauté shallots in margarine and 1 tablespoon oil over medium high heat. Add tomatoes and artichokes. Mix well. Pour mixture over chicken. Return to oven and bake for 15 minutes. Discard bay leaves. Serve over rice and couscous.

YIELD: 8 TO 10 SERVINGS

EASY CHICKEN BITES

A gourmet alternative to chicken nuggets.

¼	cup mayonnaise	1	pound boneless, skinless chicken breast halves, rinsed and cubed
¼	cup Dijon mustard		
¼	cup honey		Bread crumbs
2	tablespoons cider vinegar		

Preheat oven to 350 degrees. Blend mayonnaise, mustard, honey, and vinegar. Spread half sauce over chicken. Dredge in bread crumbs and place on a parchment paper-lined baking sheet. Bake at 350 degrees for 35 minutes. Serve with remaining half sauce.

YIELD: 6 SERVINGS

ORANGE BASIL ROAST CHICKEN

*A mere 10 minutes of prep time gives plain
ol' roasted chicken a glamorous makeover.*

1   tablespoon all-purpose flour
1   (5-7 pound) whole chicken
8   large basil leaves
1   large orange, peeled, thinly sliced,
     divided

1   medium onion, sliced
     Vegetable oil
1   teaspoon pepper

Preheat oven to 350 degrees. Shake flour into a large oven roasting bag. Place in a 13 x 9 x 2-inch baking dish. Loosen chicken breast skin using your fingers or knife handle. Place basil leaves and 4 orange slices under skin. Place half onion and half of remaining orange slices inside chicken cavity. Place remaining orange and onion slices in bottom of bag. Tuck wings under chicken and tie legs back, if desired. Brush chicken with oil. Sprinkle with pepper. Place chicken in roasting bag. Close with nylon tie. Cut six ½-inch slits in top of bag. Bake at 350 degrees for 1 hour, 15 minutes-1 hour, 30 minutes until juices run clear and chicken is tender.

YIELD: 11 TO 15 SERVINGS

POPCORN CHICKEN

*For some reason just the name "Popcorn Chicken" appeals to kids!
Juicy inside-crispy outside and small enough to "pop" in your mouth!*

½   cup all-purpose flour
¼   cup cornstarch
½   teaspoon salt
2   teaspoons baking powder
⅔   cup cold water

2   cups vegetable oil
2   pounds boneless skinless chicken
     breast halves, cut into 1 to 2-inch
     cubes
     Salt to taste

Blend flour, cornstarch, salt, baking powder, and water. Heat oil in a skillet or wok until hot. Dip chicken into batter. Drop into oil. Chicken will pop up and float on top. Cook until golden browned, crisp and cooked. Drain on paper towels. Sprinkle with salt.

YIELD: 8 SERVINGS

WHOLE CHICKEN IN A BASKET

1	onion, diced	1	teaspoon dried thyme
1	(3-4 pound) roaster	1	pound spaghetti
3	tablespoons olive oil, divided	1	tablespoon allspice
1	teaspoon season salt	1	can tomato paste
1	teaspoon lemon pepper	1	can *DonPepino* pizza sauce

Preheat oven to 400 degrees. Place diced onions in roaster. Set chicken on top and rub 2 tablespoons olive oil all over chicken and sprinkle with season salt, lemon pepper and thyme over chicken. Bake in oven for 30 minutes. Meanwhile cook spaghetti to al dente, drain, mix in remaining olive oil, allspice, tomato paste, and pizza sauce. Transfer chicken to a plate, mix spaghetti in roaster with onions and gravy. Tuck chicken in between spaghetti. Cover and bake at 300 degrees for 2 hours, 30 minutes.

SMOKY MOUNTAIN TURKEY CHILI

Here is a great opportunity to experiment with a variety of exotic peppers!
This recipe is born out of the fact that one must find something great to do with leftover turkey.
May make this using a turkey leg but leftovers allow for a shortcut. Usually turkey does not
freeze well, but it is fine to use in this recipe. It does great and the chili freezes well.

2	tablespoons vegetable oil	1	(1-3 pound) butternut squash, peeled and diced into 1-inch pieces
6	garlic cloves, minced		
2	large onions, finely chopped		
2	tablespoons ancho chile powder	2	(15 ounce) cans black beans, drained
2	tablespoons chipotle chile powder		
4	teaspoons ground cumin	4	poblano chilies, roasted, peeled and cut into ½-inch pieces
1	(28 ounce) can crushed tomatoes, undrained		Salt and pepper to taste
3-5	pounds cooked turkey, no bones	¼	(6 ounce) can tomato paste

Heat oil in large stockpot. Sauté garlic and onion. Add ancho powder, chipotle chile powder, and cumin. Cook and stir for 5 minutes. Add tomatoes with juice and simmer. Add turkey and simmer for 2 hours. Add squash and simmer for 15 minutes or until tender. Stir in black beans, poblano chilies, salt, and pepper. Stir in tomato paste until dissolved. Simmer for 30 minutes.

YIELD: 8 TO 10 SERVINGS

Poultry

TURKEY POT PIE

Easy and perfect for leftover turkey or chicken.
Puff pastry is another alternative to put on top.

2	tablespoons margarine	2	potatoes, peeled and diced
1	onion, chopped	2	cups shredded turkey
2	stalks celery, chopped	2	tablespoons chopped parsley
3	carrots, chopped	½	cup frozen peas, thawed
¼	cup all-purpose flour	1	prepared pie pastry
4	cups turkey or chicken broth	1	egg, slightly beaten

Preheat oven to 350 degrees. Melt margarine in a saucepan. Sauté onion until tender. Add celery and carrot and cook for 2 minutes. Stir in flour and cook for 2 minutes. Pour in broth. Bring to simmer. Add potatoes and simmer until tender. Add turkey, parsley and peas. Pour mixture into casserole dish. Top with pie pastry. Brush with egg. Bake at 350 degrees for 30 minutes or until golden browned.

YIELD: 6 TO 8 SERVINGS

TURKEY MEATLOAF

3	cups chopped yellow onion	¾	cup chicken broth
2	tablespoons olive oil	1½	teaspoons *DonPepino* pizza sauce
2	teaspoons kosher salt	5	pounds ground turkey breast
1	teaspoon pepper	1½	cups plain dry bread crumbs
1	teaspoon chopped thyme or ½ teaspoon dried	3	extra large eggs, beaten
⅓	cup Worcestershire sauce	¾	cup ketchup

Preheat oven to 325 degrees. Sauté onion, oil, salt, pepper, and thyme about 15 minutes until onions are translucent not browned. Add Worcestershire sauce, broth and pizza sauce. Mix well. Cool to room temperature.

Combine turkey, bread crumbs, eggs, and onion mixture in a large bowl. Mix well. Shape mixture into a loaf and place on an ungreased baking sheet. Spread ketchup evenly on top. Bake at 325 degrees for 1 hour, 30 minutes or until cooked through (internal temperature of 160 degrees). May place a pan of water in oven to avoid cracking the top. Serve hot, room temperature or cold as a sandwich.

YIELD: 8 SERVINGS

Poultry

TURKEY PICCATA

Serve with steamed rice to sop up every bit of the garlicky sauce!
You will be amazed at the turkey's similar taste to veal.

1 tablespoon plus ¼ cup lemon juice	¼ cup olive oil
1 pound turkey cutlets	2 garlic cloves, minced
½ cup all-purpose flour	½ cup white wine
1 teaspoon paprika	¼ cup chicken broth
½ teaspoon salt	2 tablespoons drained capers
½ teaspoon white pepper	Chopped parsley for garnish

Drizzle 1 tablespoon lemon juice over cutlets. Combine flour, paprika, salt, and pepper. Heat oil in a skillet. Sauté garlic for 1 minute. Dredge cutlets in flour mixture. Shake off excess and sauté in skillet 2 minutes per side until golden browned. Transfer cutlets to a serving platter and keep warm.

Blend wine, ¼ cup lemon juice and chicken broth. Pour into skillet to deglaze bottom. Bring to boil. Reduce heat and stir constantly until thickened. Add capers and cook for 1 minute. Pour sauce over cutlets. Top with parsley.

YIELD: 4 SERVINGS

TURKEY STUFFED ZUCCHINI

1 pound ground turkey	Salt, pepper, garlic and onion powder to taste
2 tablespoons raw rice	1 can *Don Pepino* pizza sauce plus ½ can water
1 egg	4 medium zucchini, cooked and halved lengthwise and scooped out (save)
2 tablespoons ketchup	
½ teaspoon Worcestershire sauce	
1½ medium onions	

Mix ground turkey with rice, egg, ketchup, Worcestershire sauce, and ½ onion grated; set aside. In a pot, add pizza sauce, water, 1 sliced onion, and inside pulp of zucchini. Bring to boil and add a dash of salt, pepper, onion, and garlic powder. Reduce heat to a simmer for about 15 minutes. Stuff meat mixture into zucchini shells. Make small meat balls with any leftover meat mixture. Place zucchini in a square casserole dish. Pour sauce mixture over the zucchini and any extra meat balls. Bake at 325 degree for 1½ hours. Baste occasionally.

152

Fish

To our favorite chef, Debby Weinstein
Thank you for sharing years of wonderful recipes and your culinary expertise with us. We love you.
Your "Chefs in Training" your children and grandchildren

Miriam Greenblatt recalls the years she and other fish mavens schlepped to Mr. Saccharin's in North Memphis to purchase kosher fish. Although Miriam has prepared her fair share of gefilte fish, she is an adventurous cook who is not opposed to breaking with tradition and trying new recipes. At her monthly Sabbath morning spreads, in honor of the new Jewish month, she would just as soon serve a July Fourth cake decorated with berries and icing as a cholent of kishka and barley. She insists that her guests come back not only for the company, but for the variety of foods she serves.

Joyce Levine learned how to cook by following a Yiddish adage that roughly translates to "just pour it in". Measurements and specific ingredients are less crucial to the success of a dish than experimentation; if you like an ingredient, it should be included in your recipe — no questions asked! Over the years, her recipes took on a Southern flair, developed by a trial and error process and yielding such gems as the "Tennessee Beef Ribs" and "Chicken with Never Fail Dumplings" included in this book.

Miriam and Joyce prove that there is more to kosher Southern fare than meets the eye. Rather than allowing their dishes to be defined by one approach, their continual quest for authentic cooking has led them to explore and perfect the myriad ways this cuisine can be interpreted.

MOROCCAN FISH

4	Yukon potatoes, peeled and sliced into ¼-inch rounds	4	(6 ounce) tilapia fillets
1	cup chickpeas	½	cup vegetable oil
3	sweet red peppers, cut into eighths	2	tablespoons paprika
8	garlic cloves, halved	1	teaspoon salt
¼	cup finely chopped cilantro	1	teaspoon ground cumin
1	lemon, peeled and sliced into rounds	1	teaspoon ground turmeric
		¼	teaspoon pepper
		1	cup water
		1	(6 ounce) can tomato paste

Layer potatoes, chickpeas, pepper, half garlic, half cilantro, and half lemon slices in a large skillet. Arrange tilapia on top. Place remaining garlic, cilantro, and lemon slices over fish. Blend oil, paprika, salt, cumin, turmeric, and pepper. Pour over fish. Blend water with tomato paste. Pour over fish. Cover and bring to boil. Reduce heat and simmer for 40 minutes.

YIELD: 4 SERVINGS

May substitute another mild flavored fish for tilapia. You do not want natural flavor of fish to compete with this dish's bold spices.

"LITE" FISH WITH VEGETABLES

A healthy and satisfying one dish family meal.

2	teaspoons butter or margarine	2	teaspoons lemon zest
4	medium carrots, peeled and cut into thin strips	1	teaspoon dried thyme
3	yellow squash, cut into thin strips	4	pieces flounder, sole, or orange roughly fillets
2	medium leeks, white part only, cut into thin strips	½	teaspoon salt
2	teaspoons lemon juice	¼	teaspoon pepper
		½	cup white wine

Preheat oven to 450 degrees. Melt butter or margarine in a greased non-stick skillet. Sauté carrot, squash and leek until crisp-tender. Add lemon juice, lemon zest, and thyme. Toss to coat. Spread vegetables into a baking dish. Sprinkle fish with salt and pepper. Arrange fish over vegetables. Pour wine over fish. Cover tightly with foil. Bake at 450 degrees for 20-25 minutes or until fish is opaque. Spoon juices over fish when serving.

YIELD: 4 SERVINGS

TILAPIA IN A COCONUT CURRY SAUCE

Curry with coconut milk is typical of Malaysian, Tamil and Bangladeshi cuisine. This dish is exotic, fragrant, easy, and delicious! This is one of those dishes that you get a craving for! Everyone loves this—kids and people who do not like curry! Great for a crowd!

2	tablespoons olive oil	2	pounds tilapia
4	cups thinly sliced yellow onions	3	teaspoons salt
2	tablespoons minced garlic	2	tablespoons light brown sugar
2	tablespoons minced ginger	1	cup julienne cut sweet red pepper
3	tablespoons curry powder	1	cup julienne cut yellow pepper
1	cup thinly sliced lemon grass, wrapped in cheesecloth	½	cup chopped cilantro plus more for garnish
4	cups parve chicken soup broth		Hot cooked rice
1	(14 ounce) can unsweetened coconut milk		

Heat oil in a Dutch oven or large stockpot over medium high heat for 5 minutes. Sauté onion, garlic and ginger for 1 minute. Add curry. Cook and stir 2 minutes until slightly toasted. Add lemon grass packet, chicken broth, and coconut milk. Bring to boil. Cook for 20 minutes or until liquid is reduced by half. Reduce heat. Sprinkle fish with salt. Add to pot. Sprinkle with brown sugar and top with peppers. Cook for 20-30 minutes or until fish is cooked. Stir in cilantro and remove from heat. Cover to keep warm. Spoon rice into large bowls. Ladle fish and curry sauce on top. Garnish with cilantro.

YIELD: 6 SERVINGS

RICE WITH INDIAN SPICES

2 tablespoons vegetable oil	1½ teaspoons mustard seeds
½ teaspoon spicy curry powder	⅔ cup raw cashew nuts
1 teaspoon turmeric	8 cups cooked rice
2-4 hot green chiles, such as jalapeño, sliced	1 lemon, juiced or to taste
	Salt

In a pot over medium heat on the stove top to warm the oil. Add the curry powder, turmeric and chiles. Cook and stir until sizzling. Add the mustard seeds and cashew nuts and cook, stirring for 5 minutes. Add the cooked rice and lemon juice and salt to taste until well combined. Put into a casserole dish and heat before serving.

Fish

156

COD, FENNEL AND POTATO CASSEROLE

*The dense texture of potatoes is a beautiful
complement to flaky fish. It is a hearty all-in-one-dish.*

2	medium fennel bulbs, stalks cut off and discarded and fronds reserved for garnish	¼	teaspoon pepper
1½	pounds large potatoes, peeled	6	tablespoons extra virgin olive oil, divided
3	large garlic cloves, minced	2	pounds skinless cod fillet, cut into 6 portions
1	teaspoon salt		

Preheat oven to 400 degrees. Cut fennel bulbs and potatoes crosswise into ¹⁄₁₆-inch thin slices. Transfer fennel and potatoes to a baking dish. Add garlic, salt, pepper, and 4 tablespoons oil. Toss to coat. Cover with foil. Bake at 400 degrees 30 minutes or until tender. Sprinkle fish with salt and pepper. Arrange fish over vegetables. Drizzle with 2 tablespoons oil. Bake, uncovered, 12-15 minutes until fish is cooked.

YIELD: 6 SERVINGS

SALMON WITH PISTACHIO, BASIL AND MINT BUTTER

The fresh herbs and nuts give the salmon an herby crust!

¼	cup shelled pistachios	1	tablespoon lemon juice
¼	cup basil leaves		Salt and pepper to taste
¼	cup mint leaves	6	(6 ounce) salmon fillets
1	garlic clove, minced	½	cup dry white wine
1	stick butter or margarine, softened		Salt and pepper to taste

Pulse pistachios, basil, mint, and garlic in a food processor until coarsely chopped. Add butter, lemon juice, salt, and pepper. Process until smooth. Refrigerate until cold. May be prepared 4 days in advance.

Preheat oven to 400 degrees. Place fillets in a single layer in a greased 13 x 9 x 2-inch baking dish. Pour on wine and sprinkle with salt and pepper. Bake at 400 degrees about 10 minutes until almost opaque. Place 2 tablespoons flavored butter on top of each fillet. Bake another 5 minutes until opaque in center. Transfer to plates and pour pan juices over fillets.

YIELD: 6 SERVINGS

APPLE AND HORSERADISH GLAZED SALMON

Sweet apple jelly and fiery horseradish swim alongside succulent salmon.

⅓ cup apple jelly

1 tablespoon finely chopped chives

2 tablespoons prepared white
    horseradish

1 tablespoon vinegar

½ teaspoon kosher salt, divided

4 (6 ounce) salmon fillets, 1-inch
    thick, skinned

¼ teaspoon pepper

2 teaspoons olive oil

Preheat oven to 350 degrees. Whisk together jelly, chives, horseradish, vinegar, and ¼ teaspoon salt. Sprinkle salmon with ¼ teaspoon salt and pepper. Heat oil in a large non-stick skillet. Add salmon and cook for 3 minutes. Turn salmon and brush with half apple mixture. Wrap skillet handle with foil. Bake at 350 degrees for 5 minutes or until fish flakes easily. Brush with remaining apple mixture.

YIELD: 4 SERVINGS

HONEY MUSTARD SALMON

This honey-kissed dish is perfect for Rosh Hashanah.

1 side of whole salmon

2 tablespoons Dijon mustard

2 tablespoons honey

1 teaspoon dried dill

1 teaspoon salt

1 teaspoon paprika

1 teaspoon ground cumin

½ teaspoon minced garlic

½ teaspoon onion powder

½ teaspoon curry powder

⅛ teaspoon cayenne pepper

Preheat broiler. Place fish on a large greased baking sheet. Spread mustard over fish. Drizzle with honey. Combine dill, salt, paprika, cumin, garlic, onion powder, curry, and cayenne. Sprinkle spice mixture over fish. Broil fish for 5 minutes. Reduce heat to 400 degrees. Bake for 15 minutes. Serve immediately, room temperature or chilled.

YIELD: 12 TO 15 SERVINGS

Fish

JACK DANIELS™ SALMON

Sugar-sauced fish with a Tennessee twist! May also be served as an appetizer!

10 (1-inch) salmon fillets
1½ cups packed brown sugar

2   cups Jack Daniels™ bourbon

Place salmon skin side down in a glass baking dish. Spread brown sugar over salmon. Pour bourbon over top. Marinate for 30 minutes. Place dish with marinade in a 400 degree oven. Bake for 25 minutes. As salmon cools, spoon bourbon-sugar sauce over fish a few times. Sauce will become a glaze at room temperature. Ladle more sauce while serving.

YIELD: 10 SERVINGS

HALIBUT OVER ARTICHOKES AND TOMATOES

4   tablespoons olive oil, divided
4   (6 ounce) halibut fillets
¼   teaspoon salt, plus more for seasoning fish
¼   teaspoon freshly ground black pepper, plus more for seasoning fish
2   shallots, sliced into thin rounds

2   cloves garlic, minced
1   pound frozen artichokes, thawed
½   cup white wine
1½ cups parve chicken broth
1   (14½ ounce) can diced tomatoes
½   teaspoon minced fresh thyme leaves

Drizzle 1 tablespoon olive oil over the halibut and season with salt and pepper. Heat a grill pan over high heat. Cook the fish on the grill pan until just cooked through, about 4 minutes per side. depending on thickness.

In a medium saucepan, heat the 3 tablespoons olive oil over medium high heat. Add the shallots and cook for 1 minute. Add the garlic and artichokes and cook until golden browned, about 5 minutes. Add the white wine and stir, scraping the brown bits off the bottom of the pan with a wooden spoon. Add the chicken broth, tomatoes and juice, thyme, and ¼ teaspoon each salt and pepper. Bring to a simmer.

Ladle the artichoke and tomato broth into shallow bowls. Top with grilled halibut. Serve immediately.

CRUNCHY "FAUX" FRIED FISH

A healthy reinvention of Southern fried fish! Typically in the South we serve our fried fish with hushpuppies. This Southern specialty is a cornmeal dumpling.

¼	cup all-purpose flour	1	teaspoon dried parsley
¼	cup cornflakes crumbs	1½-2	pounds fish (halibut or grouper)
½	tablespoon garlic powder	1	cup plain yogurt
½	teaspoon onion powder		

Combine flour, cornflakes, garlic powder, onion powder, and parsley. Dip fish in yogurt. Roll each piece in flour mixture. Bake at 400 degrees for 20-25 minutes. Broil for 2-3 minutes until browned.

YIELD: 6 SERVINGS

BUTTERMILK HUSHPUPPIES

Their name is said to have come from the fact that to keep hungry dogs from begging for food while the rest of dinner was prepared, the cooks used to toss scraps of the fried batter to them saying, "Hush puppy!"

1½	cups yellow cornmeal	1	tablespoon minced jalapeños
½	cup all-purpose flour	⅛	teaspoon cayenne pepper or more to taste
1	teaspoon baking powder	2	large eggs
½	teaspoon baking soda	½	cup buttermilk
2	teaspoons salt	½	cup water
1½	tablespoons hot red pepper sauce	6	cups vegetable oil
¼	cup minced onions	2	tablespoons Creole seasoning
¼	cup minced sweet red pepper		

Combine cornmeal, flour, baking powder, baking soda, salt, hot sauce, onion, peppers, jalapeños, and cayenne in a large bowl. Mix well. Stir in eggs, buttermilk and water. Mix well.

Heat oil in a large heavy saucepan over medium-high heat to 360 degrees. Drop batter by tablespoonfuls into hot oil. Fry about 2 minutes, turning with a long-handled spoon, until golden browned. Remove and drain on paper towels. Sprinkle with seasoning.

YIELD: 18 HUSHPUPPIES

FISH KABOBS

Kids love these as a main course too!

2 teaspoons olive oil	½ large sweet red pepper, seeded and cubed
2 tablespoons lime juice	½ large green bell pepper, seeded and cubed
1 tablespoon Dijon mustard	Cherry tomatoes
1-2 pounds fresh fish (halibut, grouper, and or cod), cut into cubes	

Combine oil, lime juice, and mustard in a small baking dish. Add fish and toss to coat. Marinate in refrigerator for at least 10 minutes. Turn fish and marinate for an additional 10 minutes. Remove fish with a slotted spoon, reserving marinade. Thread fish, pepper, and tomatoes onto skewers in alternating layers. Brush kabobs with reserved marinade.

Place skewers on a broiler pan. Broil about 4 inches from heat source for 3-5 minutes. Turn skewers and brush with marinade. Broil until fish is cooked and vegetables are crisp-tender.

YIELD: 6 TO 8 SERVINGS

SAFFRON RICE

¼ teaspoon saffron thread	3 tablespoons salad oil
3 chicken bouillon cubes	1 cup uncooked rice
2½ cups boiling water	⅓ cup seedless raisins
⅛ teaspoon garlic powder	3 tablespoons slivered almonds
Sprinkling of fresh ground pepper	

Dissolve saffron and bouillon cubes in boiling water. Put into casserole dish. Add garlic, pepper, and salad oil. Mix in rice and raisins. Cover and bake at 350 degrees for about 45 minutes or until rice is tender. Add almonds during the last 10 minutes of baking.

LOW-FAT BAKED SALMON CROQUETTES

An updated and healthier version of the traditionally fried classic!

2   (6 ounce) cans boneless skinless salmon
Soymilk or milk
4   tablespoons butter or margarine
2   tablespoons finely chopped onion
⅓   cup all-purpose flour

½   teaspoon salt
¼   teaspoon pepper
1   tablespoon lemon juice
1   cup crushed cornflake crumbs, divided

Drain salmon, reserving liquid. Add enough milk to salmon liquid to measure 1 cup. Melt butter or margarine in a saucepan over low heat. Sauté onion until tender. Stir in flour until smooth. Cook 1 minute, stirring constantly. Gradually stir in milk mixture until thickened and bubbly. Add salt and pepper.

In a separate bowl, combine salmon, lemon juice, ½ cup cornflake crumbs, and white sauce. Refrigerate for 30 minutes. Shape mixture into croquettes and roll in ½ cup cornflake crumbs. Place on a greased baking sheet or baking dish. Bake at 400 degrees for 30 minutes.

YIELD: 6 SERVINGS

TARTAR SAUCE

1 cup mayonnaise

2 tablespoons dill pickle relish

2 tablespoons capers, drained and rinsed

2 tablespoons chopped chives

1 tablespoon chopped tarragon

1 tablespoon Dijon mustard

2 teaspoons lemon juice

¼ teaspoon pepper

Blend mayonnaise, relish, capers, chives, tarragon, mustard, lemon juice, and pepper until smooth. Cover and refrigerate until ready to serve.

SALMON PATTIES

They eat them right out of the frying pans! Make plenty!

2   (7 ounce) packages vacuum packed salmon, drained and flaked
2   large eggs, beaten
⅔   cup buttery round cracker crumbs, divided
1   small onion, finely chopped
1   tablespoon lemon juice
¼   teaspoon salt
½   teaspoon pepper
1   cup vegetable oil

Combine salmon, eggs, ⅓ cup cracker crumbs, onion, lemon juice, salt, and pepper. Mix well. Shape mixture into 4-inch patties. Coat patties in remaining cracker crumbs. Place patties well apart on a parchment paper-lined tray. Refrigerate at least 30 minutes. Fry patties in hot oil over medium heat until browned. Turn once and fry until crisp. Drain on paper towels.

YIELD: 4 TO 6 SERVINGS

May double or triple recipe to make about 20 patties. May substitute 2 (7½ ounce) cans for packages.

BAKED HALIBUT STEAKS

1   teaspoon olive oil
1   cup diced zucchini
½   cup minced onion
1   clove garlic, peeled and minced
2   cups diced fresh tomatoes
2   tablespoons chopped fresh basil
¼   teaspoon salt
¼   teaspoon ground black pepper
4   (6 ounce) halibut steaks
⅓   cup crumbled feta cheese

Preheat oven to 450 degrees. Lightly grease a medium baking dish. Heat olive oil in a medium saucepan over medium heat, and stir in zucchini, onion, and garlic. Cook and stir 5 minutes or until tender. Remove saucepan from heat, and mix in tomatoes, basil, salt, and pepper. Arrange halibut steaks in a single layer in the prepared baking dish. Spoon equal amounts of the zucchini mixture over each steak. Top with feta cheese. Bake 15 minutes in preheated oven, or until fish is easily flaked with a fork.

YIELD: 4 SERVINGS

SOUTH OF THE BORDER SNAPPER

Lime juice, dates, and coriander seeds
conspire to create a unique and scrumptious flavor.

1	onion, chopped	½	cup lime juice
1	tablespoon coriander seeds	½	cup dry white wine
1	tablespoon cumin seeds	1	cup chopped sweet red pepper
	Pinch of cayenne pepper	2	tomatoes, chopped
¼	cup olive oil	1	(2 pound) whole red snapper
½	cup chopped dates		

Preheat oven to 375 degrees. Sauté onion, coriander, cumin, and cayenne in oil in a saucepan for 5 minutes. Stir in dates, lime juice, wine, pepper, and tomatoes. Bring to boil. Remove from heat.

Rinse fish and pat dry. Place in a deep greased baking dish. Pour sauce over fish. Bake at 375 degrees for 30 minutes or until fish flakes easily.

YIELD: 6 SERVINGS

HORSERADISH ENCRUSTED GROUPER

Horseradish, long celebrated in Jewish cooking, is a member
of the same botanical family as mustard and cabbages.

6	eggs, beaten	8	(4 ounce) grouper fillets
1	(4 ounce) jar prepared white horseradish	2	cups plain bread crumbs
	Salt and pepper to taste	4	tablespoons butter or margarine

Whisk together eggs, horseradish, salt, and pepper. Dip fillets in horseradish mixture. Dredge in bread crumbs. Heat butter or margarine in a skillet over medium heat. Sauté fish on both sides until golden browned.

YIELD: 8 SERVINGS

SPICE CRUSTED TUNA

This unique and creative approach gives new excitement to tuna steaks.

¼	cup ground fennel		Salt and pepper to taste
¼	cup ground coriander	1	pound tuna fillets
¼	cup ground mustard	2	tablespoons olive oil
3	tablespoons sugar		Oil for frying

Combine fennel, coriander, mustard, sugar, salt, and pepper. Dip tuna in oil. Press spice mixture onto tuna on all sides. Heat oil in skillet. Fry tuna about 5 minutes per side. Put relish on top of each tuna steak to serve.

YIELD: 4 SERVINGS

SAVORY GREEN RICE

1 bunch Italian flat leaf parsley	6 garlic cloves, minced
1 bunch cilantro	1 teaspoon ginger, minced
1 green pepper	Olive oil
1 hot chili pepper	1½ cups rice
1 bunch green onions	3½ cups water

Purée parsley, cilantro, green pepper, chili pepper, and green onions. Sauté garlic and ginger in a little olive oil over medium heat. Add dry rice to garlic and ginger and turn up the heat. Combine green mixture and water. Pour over rice and bring to a boil, cover and lower heat for 20-25 minutes or until rice is tender.

Pair this Savory Green Rice with the Tenderloin Roast with Jezebel Sauce for a spectacularly colored meal with rich flavors.

HONEY SWEET CURRANT COD

Pungent ingredients and overnight marinating give this fish its bold flavor.

½ teaspoon cinnamon	Pinch of salt
½ teaspoon pepper	¼ cup olive oil, divided
½ teaspoon Aleppo pepper (red pepper)	1½ pounds cod fillets
Pinch of ground nutmeg	3 tablespoons currants
Pinch of ground turmeric	1 onion, chopped
Pinch of ground cardamom	¼ cup wine vinegar
Pinch of ground ginger	2 tablespoons chopped parsley
Pinch of ground cloves	¼ cup honey

Combine cinnamon, pepper, red pepper, nutmeg, turmeric, cardamom, ginger, cloves, salt, and 2 tablespoons oil. Brush marinade sparingly on fillets, reserve remaining marinade. Cover and marinate fish at least 2 hours or overnight.

Preheat oven to 350 degrees. Soak currants in water. Sauté onion in 2 tablespoons oil until tender. Drain currants and add to onions. Stir in reserved marinade, vinegar, parsley, and honey. Reduce heat and simmer 10 minutes or until liquid is reduced. Bake fish at 350 degrees until almost done. Spoon sauce on top of fish. Cover and bake an additional 10 minutes until tender.

YIELD: 6 SERVINGS

PICKLED SWEET AND SOUR SALMON

6 pounds salmon, filleted (a side of a whole salmon)	2 onions, sliced
	¼ cup vinegar

MARINADE

2 cups vinegar	1½ cups ketchup
2 cups sugar	

Place salmon in a glass dish with water to cover and ¼ cup vinegar. Poach salmon in a 400 degree oven for 15-20 minutes. Mix marinade in a separate bowl. Put a layer of onions over and under poached salmon and pour marinade over the salmon. Cover tightly and refrigerate for 2-3 days. Will keep for up to 10 days or more.

Note: You may add pickling spices to water in the poaching process, or add to the marinade.

Fish

FRIED CURRY FISH

You will want to make this fish again and again with this sauce poured over it.

CURRY SAUCE

2   cups vinegar
1   cup water
4   onions, sliced
5-8 peppercorns

10 bay leaves
1   cup sugar
2   teaspoons curry powder

CURRY SAUCE

Combine vinegar, water, onion, peppercorns, and bay leaves in a saucepan. Bring to boil. In a separate bowl, combine sugar and curry powder. Stir into onion mixture. Boil for 10 minutes. Reduce heat and keep warm.

FISH

3   pounds fish fillets
    (tilapia or cod)
    All-purpose flour

3   eggs
1   teaspoon lemon juice
    Vegetable oil

FISH

Cut fish into portion size pieces. Dredge each piece in flour. Blend eggs and lemon juice. Dip fish in egg mixture and then dredge in flour again. Heat oil in a skillet. Fry fish, turning once, until done. Arrange fish in a casserole dish. Pour warm sauce over fish and serve.

YIELD: 8 SERVINGS

This sauce may be cooled and refrigerated. It will keep for several weeks.

SALMON TUNA LOAF

2   (6 ounce) cans tuna, undrained
2   (6 ounce) cans boneless skinless
    salmon, undrained
½   cup seasoned bread crumbs

1   egg, beaten
¾   cup shredded Cheddar cheese
¾   teaspoon pepper
3   tablespoons butter, melted

Combine tuna, salmon, bread crumbs, egg, Cheddar cheese, pepper, and butter. Mix well. Shape mixture into a loaf. Place in a greased 13 x 9 x 2-inch baking dish. Bake at 350 degrees for 30 minutes.

YIELD: 4 TO 6 SERVINGS

FLOUNDER FLORENTINE

Florentine refers to a dish made with spinach and cheese.
This fish looks and sounds fancy, but it is light in calories and easy to make.

½ cup chopped onion	2 tablespoons lemon juice
2 garlic cloves, minced	2 tablespoons mayonnaise
1½ cups sliced mushrooms	1 teaspoon Dijon mustard
1½ cups well drained frozen spinach	2-3 tablespoons grated Parmesan cheese
Salt and pepper to taste	
4 flounder fillets	1 tablespoon dried parsley

Preheat oven to 400 degrees. Sauté onions and garlic in a greased non-stick skillet until tender. Add mushrooms and cook until liquid is evaporated. Add spinach, salt, and pepper. Spoon equal portions of spinach mixture onto center of each fillet. Roll up fillet to enclose filling. Place seam side down in a shallow casserole dish. Drizzle with lemon juice. Blend mayonnaise and mustard. Spread evenly over fish rolls. Sprinkle with Parmesan cheese. Bake at 400 degrees about 20 minutes or until lightly browned. Garnish with parsley.

YIELD: 4 SERVINGS

BLACKENED TUNA

6-8 tuna fillets	½ teaspoon garlic powder
1 teaspoon crushed dried thyme leaves	½ teaspoon onion powder
1 teaspoon cayenne pepper	½ teaspoon paprika
1 teaspoon black pepper	½ cup butter, melted
1 teaspoon salt	Lemon juice

Make seasoning mixture by combining crushed dried thyme leaves, cayenne pepper, black pepper, salt, garlic powder, onion powder, and paprika in a small bowl.

Brush melted butter lightly over tuna fillets and sprinkle with blackened seasoning mix. Repeat for other side. Be sure to completely coat each fillet.

Heat skillet until it is very hot, about 10 minutes. Pour the leftover butter into your skillet. Carefully place the tuna fillets into the skillet and cook for about 4 minutes on both sides. This blackened seasoning mixture will produce some smoke so another way to tell when to turn over fillets is when the smoke turns gray. Serve finished fillets over a bed of white steamed rice.

Vegetables & Side Dishes

When our fields are cultivated and well tended, the land bears beautiful fruit.
So, too, when the school nurtures and cares for our nieces and nephews,
it brings forth a beautiful child.
Joyce and David Krasner

Memphis traditions are often passed down several generations, changing little with the passage of time. For the Thomas family, it begins with Bettie Thomas, whose home sometimes swelled with dozens of people invited to partake in a fabulous meal presented with extraordinary Southern charm. For Ricki Krupp, Bettie's daughter, her mother's inspired flair translated into a deep love for baking, which motivated her to create her signature chipstick cookie. After baking cookies for several years, Ricki branched out into challah making, impelled by a desire to ensure that fresh challahs were always available. Thursday nights became challah-baking night in the Krupp house, and Ricki couldn't set the table for the Sabbath until the challahs were gone. "I still have the 12 foot-long table that I used to line up the challahs that were destined for other people's Friday night dinners in 1992," Ricki remembers fondly. Since 2000, Ricki has been selling chipsticks, challahs and other baked goods from her bakery, Ricki's Cookie Corner. Fortunately, she can set her table on Thursday mroning before going into the store to bake 400 challahs. These days, she is lucky to come home with a challah for her own table!

SIGNATURE EGGPLANT PARMESAN

2 small eggplants, peeled and sliced into ½-inch pieces

Salt

1 (16 ounce) container cottage cheese

2 eggs

¼ cup grated Parmesan cheese

¼ cup chopped Italian parsley

½ cup olive oil

2 cups *DonPeping* pizza sauce

2¼ cups shredded mozzarella cheese

Place eggplant in a colander. Sprinkle with salt. Allow to drain for 30 minutes. Rinse eggplant and pat dry. Combine cottage cheese, eggs, Parmesan cheese, and parsley. Heat oil in a skillet. Fry eggplant in oil until lightly browned and crisp on both sides. Spread 1 cup pizza sauce in bottom of baking dish. Layer half eggplant slices, cottage cheese mixture, and mozzarella cheese. Repeat layers of pizza sauce, eggplant, cottage cheese mixture, and mozzarella cheese. Bake at 400 degrees for 30 minutes or until bubbly. Cool 5 minutes before serving.

YIELD: 6 TO 8 SERVINGS

DIXIE DEVILED EGGS

Great as a side dish for any meal! This basic recipe is a Southern classic, but find ways to spin it into your own personal specialty. Horseradish, olives, caviar, or green onion are great ingredients to experiment with, as are spices, such as, dill, chives and cayenne.

12 hard-cooked eggs, halved

5 tablespoons mayonnaise

2 tablespoons sweet relish

1 teaspoon seasoned salt

2 teaspoons Dijon mustard

¼ teaspoon Worcestershire sauce

Paprika to taste

Scoop out yolk and place in a bowl. Arrange egg white on a platter. Blend yolks, mayonnaise, relish, seasoned salt, mustard, and Worcestershire sauce. Mix well. Add more mayonnaise to reach good consistency. Spoon a heaping teaspoonful to fill egg whites. Lightly sprinkle with paprika.

YIELD: 10 TO 12 SERVINGS

CORN PUDDING

Just like Bubbe used to make it!

2	(14 ounce) cans cream style corn	1	tablespoon vanilla
1	cup sugar	3	tablespoons all-purpose flour
4	tablespoons margarine, melted	5	eggs

Combine corn, sugar, margarine, vanilla, flour, and eggs. Mix well. Pour mixture into a 13 x 9 x 2-inch baking dish. Bake at 350 degrees for 45 minutes or until golden browned and set.

YIELD: 8 TO 10 SERVINGS

MEMPHIS-STYLE BAKED BEANS

The recipe standard for the classic baked beans.
It does not get more Southern than this, y'all.

1	(28 ounce) can vegetarian baked beans	⅓	cup sauerkraut
¼	cup packed brown sugar	2	tablespoons hickory smoke flavored barbeque sauce
2	tablespoons spicy mustard		French fried onion rings

Preheat oven to 350 degrees. Combine baked beans, brown sugar, mustard, sauerkraut, and barbecue sauce. Pour into a casserole dish. Cover with onion rings. Bake at 350 degrees for 30 minutes.

YIELD: 4 SERVINGS

CORN FRITTERS

What is a fritter? It is Southern for "let me have some more!"

Vegetable oil
4 tablespoons margarine
1 cup soymilk
2 eggs
1¼ cups self-rising cornmeal mix

1¼ cups all-purpose flour
¼ cup sugar
1 teaspoon salt
2 cups fresh, frozen or canned corn

Heat oil in a skillet or Dutch oven. Melt margarine in a bowl. Beat in soymilk and eggs. Stir in cornmeal, flour, sugar, salt, and corn. Mix well. Spoon heaping tablespoonfuls into hot oil. Cook 2-4 minutes on each side until golden browned. Drain on paper towels.

YIELD: 8 SERVINGS

GRILLED CORN WITH LIME ZEST AND CRACKED BLACK PEPPER

A great side, but also suitable for a cold salad.

6 ears corn
2 tablespoons olive oil
Salt to taste
3 tablespoons margarine

Zest of 1 lime
Juice of 1 lime
1 tablespoon cracked black pepper

Brush corn with oil and sprinkle with salt. Grill until lightly golden browned on all sides. Cut corn from cob. Melt margarine in a skillet. Add corn, lime zest and lime juice. Cook for 2-3 minutes. Add pepper.

YIELD: 6 SERVINGS

To short cut this recipe, roast corn in the oven. May also use canned or frozen corn. Brown corn in oil over medium-high heat for 5 minutes. Add remaining ingredients.

CARAMELIZED ONIONS AND PECAN GREEN BEANS

Two savory delights from the garden in one easy dish!

2 pounds green beans	1 tablespoon sugar
4 tablespoons margarine	1 teaspoon salt
1 cup coarsely chopped pecans	½ teaspoon pepper
1 large onion, halved and thinly sliced	

Bring pot of water to boil. Add green beans and cook 5 minutes. Drain and plunge into ice water. Green beans will be al dente.

Melt margarine in a large skillet over medium high heat. Sauté pecans about 5 minutes until toasted. Remove from skillet with a slotted spoon. Add onion to skillet. Cook and stir 15 minutes until caramel colored. Stir in sugar. Return pecans and add green beans. Add salt and pepper. Cook 5 more minutes.

YIELD: 6 SERVINGS

SPICY SOUTHERN GREEN BEANS

To ensure tenderness, never choose fresh green beans that are thicker in diameter than a pencil.

1 pound green beans	1 teaspoon sherry
1 teaspoon soy sauce	1 tablespoon vegetable oil
1 teaspoon sesame oil	1 tablespoon minced garlic
1 teaspoon chili paste	1 tablespoon chopped ginger
1 teaspoon honey	

Steam green beans for 3 minutes. Plunge into ice water. Whisk together soy sauce, sesame oil, chili sauce, honey, and sherry. Heat oil in skillet until hot. Sauté garlic and ginger for 30 seconds. Add green beans and cook 1-2 minutes. Pour in soy sauce mixture and cook 1-2 minutes. Serve hot.

YIELD: 6 SERVINGS

LIMA BEAN CASSEROLE

This casserole is great year round!

1 cup mayonnaise
2 tablespoons vegetable oil
1 (16 ounce) package frozen lima beans, cooked and drained
1 (15 ounce) can green beans, drained
1 (8 ounce) can sliced water chestnuts, drained

1 (15 ounce) can green peas, drained
½ cup chopped onions
½ cup plain bread crumbs
¼ teaspoon garlic powder
½ teaspoon seasoned salt
½ tablespoon dry onion soup mix
Salt and pepper to taste

Blend mayonnaise and oil. Add lima beans, green beans, water chestnuts, peas, and onion. Spoon mixture into a greased casserole dish. Combine bread crumbs, garlic powder, seasoned salt, soup mix, salt, and pepper. Spread mixture over bean mixture. Bake at 350 degrees for 30-45 minutes.

YIELD: 8 TO 10 SERVINGS

MAMA'S SWEET POTATO PIE

In some homes, this versatile Southern classic is served as dessert instead of a side dish.

1 (15 ounce) can sweet potatoes, mashed
¾ cup soymilk
¾ cup firmly packed brown sugar
2 large eggs

1 tablespoon margarine, melted
½ teaspoon salt
½ teaspoon cinnamon
1 (9 inch) pie shell, unbaked

Preheat oven to 400 degrees. Blend potatoes, soymilk, brown sugar, eggs, margarine, salt, and cinnamon with a mixer until smooth. Pour mixture into pie shell. Bake at 400 degrees for 10 minutes. Reduce heat to 350 degrees. Bake an additional 35 minutes or until tester comes out clean. After 20 minutes, cover edges with foil to prevent excess browning.

YIELD: 8 SERVINGS

BOURBON PECAN TOPPED SWEET POTATOES

What do you get when you mix pecans, bourbon, and sweet potatoes? A Southern-style triple treat!

POTATOES

4-5	sweet potatoes	⅔	cup soymilk
1	cup sugar	1	teaspoon vanilla
3	eggs	2	tablespoons bourbon
1	stick margarine, melted		

POTATOES

Cook and mash sweet potatoes. Add sugar, eggs, margarine, soymilk, vanilla, and bourbon. Mix well. Pour mixture into a well-greased casserole dish.

TOPPING

1	cup chopped pecans	1	cup all-purpose flour
1	cup packed brown sugar	1	stick margarine, softened

TOPPING

Combine pecans, brown sugar, flour, and margarine. Sprinkle over potatoes. Bake at 350 degrees for 40 minutes.

YIELD: 4 TO 6 SERVINGS

NICE' N' HOT APRICOTS

A sweet side dish that is a perfect pairing for fish and chicken.

2	(16 ounce) cans peeled apricots		Cracker crumbs
	Light brown sugar	4	tablespoons margarine, softened
3	tablespoons lemon juice		

Drain apricot for 1 hour. Place apricots center cut up in a glass dish. Sprinkle with brown sugar and lemon juice. Refrigerate overnight.

Just before baking, sprinkle with cracker crumbs and dot with margarine. Bake at 350 degrees for 40-45 minutes.

YIELD: 4 TO 6 SERVINGS

CRANBERRY PIE

A great side dish, but when you add a scoop
of ice cream, it is a terrific sweet-and-tart dessert!

FILLING

1 (12 ounce) package cranberries	¼ cup packed light brown sugar
½ cup chopped walnuts	½ teaspoon cinnamon
¼ cup sugar	1 (9 inch) frozen pie shell

FILLING

Combine cranberries, walnuts, sugar, brown sugar, and cinnamon. Spoon mixture into pie shell.

TOPPING

1 egg	4 tablespoons margarine, softened
⅓ cup sugar	3 tablespoons all-purpose flour

TOPPING

Whip together egg, sugar, margarine, and flour until smooth. Spread over filling. Bake at 400 degrees for 20 minutes. Reduce temperature to 350 degrees. Bake an additional 30 minutes.

YIELD: 8 SERVINGS

BRANDIED FALL FRUIT

A kicky fruity side dish when you are longing for summery warmth!

1	(20 ounce) can sliced pineapple, drained and halved	1	stick margarine	
1	(16 ounce) can peach halves, drained and halved	½	cup packed light brown sugar	
1	(29 ounce) can pear halves, drained, and halved	2	tablespoons all-purpose flour	
1	(16 ounce) can apricot halves, drained and halved	¼	cup frozen orange juice, thawed	
		½	cup brandy	

Arrange fruit in alternating layers in a greased casserole dish. Combine margarine, brown sugar, flour, and orange juice in a double boiler. Cook and stir until smooth and thickened. Add brandy. Pour sauce over fruit. Cover and refrigerate overnight. Remove from refrigerator 1 hour before baking. Bake at 350 degrees for 20 minutes.

YIELD: 10 SERVINGS

PLUM PUDDING

A yummy treat that is almost like a cobbler!

1	cup all-purpose flour	1	teaspoon vanilla
1	cup sugar	½	teaspoon baking powder
½	cup vegetable oil	1	(21 ounce) can peach pie filling
3	eggs	1	(16 ounce) can plums, drained

Combine flour, sugar, oil, eggs, vanilla, and baking powder. Pour half batter into a greased 9 x 9 x 2-inch baking dish. Spoon peach filling on top. Arrange plums over peach filling. Pour remaining batter over fruit. Bake at 350 degrees for 40-45 minutes.

YIELD: 8 SERVINGS

ASPARAGUS WITH TOMATOES, PINE NUTS AND BASIL

The contrasting colors and textures in this dish provide opportunity for beautiful and creative presentation. Cascade the tomato, pine nut, basil, and shallot relish over the asparagus.

2	pounds asparagus, trimmed
¼	cup olive oil
1	tablespoon olive oil
1	tablespoon balsamic vinegar
¼	cup coarsely chopped basil
2	plum tomatoes, finely chopped
1	shallot, chopped
¼	cup pine nuts, toasted

Place asparagus in a pot. Pour in water to just cover. Bring to boil. Reduce heat and simmer for 5-7 minutes. Drain and immediately plunge into cold water. Whisk together ¼ cup oil, vinegar, and basil. Sauté shallots in 1 tablespoon oil. Add tomatoes, shallots, and pine nuts to dressing. Arrange asparagus on a platter. Spoon dressing over bottom half of asparagus.

YIELD: 6 SERVINGS

MARINATED ASPARAGUS

The warm spices combine with vinegar for a tangy aromatic marinade. Do not try to figure out how these ingredients can possibly come together-just make it!

2	(15 ounce) cans asparagus, or 1 bunch fresh, steamed	1	cup white vinegar
1	cup sugar	10	whole cloves
1	cup water	3	sticks cinnamon
		2	teaspoons celery seeds

Drain asparagus and arrange in a 13 x 9 x 2-inch baking dish. Combine sugar, water, vinegar, cloves, cinnamon, and celery seed in a saucepan. Bring to boil. Cook until sugar dissolves. Cool for 5 minutes. Strain marinade over asparagus. Discard cloves and cinnamon sticks. Cover and refrigerate at least 2 hours or overnight.

YIELD: 6 SERVINGS

ASPARAGUS, PEAS AND CASHEWS

Easy, elegant, and earthy!

1   stick margarine
¼   cup lemon juice
½   cup chopped cashews

2   (10 ounce) packages frozen peas, cooked and drained
2   (15 ounce) cans asparagus, drained

Heat margarine, lemon juice, and cashews in saucepan until margarine melts. Combine peas and asparagus in a casserole dish. Pour margarine sauce over top. Bake at 350 degrees until thoroughly heated.

YIELD: 8 SERVINGS

CREAMY BROCCOLI SOUFFLÉ

Broccoli is more than just delicious! It is loaded with calcium, fiber and vitamins A,C and K!

2   tablespoons dry onion soup mix, divided
1   (10 ounce) package frozen broccoli or cauliflower (optional)
1½ tablespoons margarine

1½ tablespoons all-purpose flour
½   cup soymilk
3   eggs, beaten
½   cup mayonnaise
½   cup cornflake crumbs

Sprinkle 1 tablespoon onion soup mix on top of frozen broccoli. Cook in microwave according to package directions. Drain broccoli and set aside. Melt margarine in a saucepan. Whisk in flour until smooth. Add soymilk and stir until thickened. Remove from heat and set aside.

Beat together eggs, mayonnaise, and 1 tablespoon onion soup mix. Add broccoli to mixture. Gently fold in margarine sauce. Spread half cornflake crumbs on bottom of a greased 8 x 8 x 2-inch baking dish. Pour broccoli mixture over top. Sprinkle with remaining cornflake crumbs. Bake at 350 degrees for 30 minutes.

YIELD: 4 TO 6 SERVINGS

BROCCOLI RICE CASSEROLE

Makes a lot for a big crowd and is great to freeze!

TOPPING

1½ cups mayonnaise

2 tablespoons grated onion

TOPPING

Combine mayonnaise and onion until smooth. Set aside.

BROCCOLI

1 cup rice

1 (15 ounce) can chicken broth

1 tablespoon chicken bouillon granules

½ cup water

4 eggs

½ cup soymilk

1 medium onion, grated

1½ cups mayonnaise

1 (8 ounce) can water chestnuts, drained and sliced

1 (10¾ ounce) can cream of mushroom soup

2 (16 ounce) packages frozen cut broccoli

Paprika to taste

BROCCOLI

Cook rice, broth, bouillon, and water until liquid is absorbed. Cool. Beat eggs until light and fluffy. Add soymilk, onion, mayonnaise, chestnuts, and mushroom soup. Mix well. Add rice. Defrost broccoli and add to mixture. Pour mixture into a greased 13 x 9 x 2-inch baking dish. Bake at 350 degrees for 50 minutes or until broccoli is done. Remove from oven. Spread topping over broccoli. Sprinkle with paprika. Return to oven and bake until browned.

YIELD: 10 TO 12 SERVINGS

SPICY ROASTED BROCCOLI

¼ cup olive oil

1 tablespoon chili powder

5 garlic cloves, minced

1 tablespoon grilled seasoning

1 bunch fresh broccoli, cut into florets

Whisk together oil, chili powder, garlic, and seasoning. Pour over broccoli. Place broccoli on a baking sheet. Bake at 425 degrees for 17-20 minutes.

YIELD: 4 SERVINGS

BAKED BROCCOLI

Tender broccoli cloaked in a savory, tangy sauce with a touch of crunchiness.

1	bunch broccoli	2	tablespoons Dijon mustard
½	cup mayonnaise	¾	cup French fried onion rings

Preheat oven to 350 degrees. Cut broccoli stems so that top will stand up next to each together in a dish. Pour in ¼-inch water. Cover tightly with plastic wrap. Microwave for 7 minutes. Blend mayonnaise and mustard in a separate bowl. Uncover broccoli and spread mayonnaise mixture over broccoli. Top with onion rings. Bake at 350 degrees for 30 minutes.

YIELD: 4 SERVINGS

How hard can this recipe be with four ingredients? Easy and delicious — don't let it slip by as one of your staple side dishes!

ORANGE-SPIKED BRUSSELS SPROUTS AND CAULIFLOWER

A sunny spin on winter vegetables.

1	large head cauliflower, cut into florets	2	teaspoons minced garlic
1	pound Brussels sprouts, larger ones halved	1	tablespoon orange zest
			Salt and pepper to taste
⅓	cup olive oil	½	cup orange juice
¼	cup chopped shallots	⅓	cup chopped Italian parsley
			Orange sliced for garnish

Preheat oven to 450 degrees. Combine cauliflower, sprouts, oil, shallots, garlic, and zest. Toss to coat. Place mixture in a glass baking dish. Sprinkle with salt and pepper. Roast at 450 degrees for 15 minutes or until tender and lightly browned. Pour on orange juice. Roast an additional 8 minutes until juice is evaporated. Stir in parsley and garnish with orange slices.

YIELD: 6 SERVINGS

CHEESY WHOLE BAKED CAULIFLOWER

The whole head of cauliflower offers opportunities for dramatic presentation.

1 head cauliflower or broccoli	1-2 teaspoons minced onion
¼ cup water	1 teaspoon Dijon mustard
½ cup mayonnaise	1 cup shredded Cheddar cheese

Steam cauliflower in water for 5 minutes until tender. Place cauliflower in a casserole dish. Blend mayonnaise, onion, and mustard. Spread mixture evenly over cauliflower. Press Cheddar cheese on top of cauliflower. Bake at 350 degrees about 20-25 minutes or until cheese melts.

YIELD: 6 SERVINGS

Place cauliflower on a platter surrounded by fish or make it the centerpiece of a warm vegetable platter.

CABBAGE WITH COUNTRY MUSTARD AND HORSERADISH

Light in calories, high in fiber and flavor! The robust flavors of mustard and horseradish are perfect complements to savory cabbage.

3 tablespoons margarine	1 cup water, divided
1 large onion, thinly sliced	1 tablespoon country-style coarse grain mustard
2-2½ pounds green cabbage, quartered, cored and cut into ½-inch slices	2 tablespoons white horseradish
¾ teaspoon salt	1 tablespoon all-purpose flour
	Salt and pepper to taste

Melt margarine in a heavy skillet over medium high heat. Sauté onion 5-10 minutes until lightly browned. Add cabbage, salt, and ½ cup water. Cook and stir 10-15 minutes or until cabbage is tender. Transfer cabbage to a plate. Whisk together mustard, horseradish, and flour in the skillet. Whisk in ½ cup water. Simmer for 2-3 minutes. Return cabbage, add salt and pepper, and heat thoroughly.

YIELD: 6 TO 8 SERVINGS

GINGERED CARROTS AND PARSNIPS

Parsnips and carrots are soul mates! A sprinkle of raisins makes a great garnish.

3   tablespoons olive oil

2   teaspoons minced garlic

1   tablespoon chopped ginger

3-4 carrots, peeled and sliced into
¼-inch rounds

3-4 parsnips, peeled and sliced into
¼-inch rounds

¼   teaspoon kosher salt

⅛   teaspoon pepper

Heat 2 tablespoons oil in a skillet. Sauté garlic and ginger for 30 seconds-1 minute. Stir in carrot and parsnip until coated. Add 1 tablespoon oil, salt, and pepper. Reduce heat, cover and simmer until vegetables are tender, stirring occasionally.

YIELD: 6 TO 8 SERVINGS

CARROT SOUFFLÉ

A guarantee that your kids will eat their carrots!

3   egg whites

3   egg yolks

½   cup sugar

½   cup vegetable oil

½   cup soymilk

½   cup all-purpose flour

3   teaspoons baking powder
Dash of lemon juice

1   teaspoon vanilla

½   teaspoon salt

2   cups shredded carrots

Beat egg whites until stiff. Mix egg yolks, sugar, oil, milk, flour, baking powder, lemon juice, vanilla, salt, and carrot. Fold into egg whites. Pour mixture into a greased soufflé dish. Bake at 350 degrees for 1 hour.

YIELD: 6 SERVINGS

BABY CARROTS WITH ROSEMARY AND FENNEL

A simple and aromatic alternative to ordinary cooked carrots!

2 pounds baby carrots
1 fennel bulb, thinly sliced

2 tablespoons chopped rosemary
Salt and pepper to taste
1 stick margarine, cut into pieces

Preheat oven to 400 degrees. Combine carrot, fennel, and rosemary. Sprinkle with salt and pepper. Pour mixture into a greased 13 x 9 x 2-inch baking dish. Dot with margarine. Roast at 400 degrees for 30-45 minutes, stirring frequently.

YIELD: 8 TO 10 SERVINGS

CARROT RING

Cornflake crumbs
1 cup vegetable shortening
½ cup packed brown sugar
1 egg
1½ cups grated carrots
1¼ cups all-purpose flour

1 teaspoon baking powder
Pinch of salt
1 teaspoon lemon juice
½ teaspoon baking soda
1 tablespoon cold water

Sprinkle cornflake crumbs in the bottom of a greased ring mold. Cream shortening, brown sugar, egg, and carrot. Sift together flour, baking powder, and salt. Add to egg mixture. Stir in lemon juice. Dissolve baking soda in cold water. Add to carrot mixture. Pour mixture into ring mold. Top with cornflake crumbs. Bake at 350 degrees for 45-60 minutes.

YIELD: 6 SERVINGS

POTATO PARSNIP LATKES

1   large baking potato, peeled and shredded
1   tablespoon lemon juice
2   parsnips, peeled and shredded or julienne cut
¼   cup all-purpose flour

2   large eggs, slightly beaten
3   teaspoons finely chopped chives
¾   teaspoon salt
¼   teaspoon pepper
¾   cup vegetable oil

Preheat oven to 250 degrees. Combine potato and lemon juice, tossing to coat. Place potato on a towel and squeeze all liquid from potato. Mix together potato, parsnip, flour, eggs, chives, salt, and pepper. Heat oil in a skillet over medium high heat. Spoon heaping tablespoonfuls of mixture into skillet and press flat. Cook 2-3 minutes on each side until golden browned. Transfer to a paper towel-lined plate. Keep warm in oven.

YIELD: 4 SERVINGS

HOMEMADE APPLESAUCE

It is not just for babies anymore! The homemade version puts a sophisticated spin on the jarred staple in every pantry. Give it your own touch by experimenting with additional spices, such as, nutmeg and cloves.

3 pounds mixed apples, cored and quartered

½ cup water

1 cup sugar

Juice of ½ lemon

2 teaspoons cinnamon (optional)

Combine apples, water, sugar, lemon juice, and cinnamon in a large saucepan on medium-high heat. Bring to boil. Reduce heat and simmer 20 minutes, stirring frequently to break up apples. Apple will be tender and chunky. Simmer until apples are desired consistency. Serve warm or cold.

YIELD: 6 TO 8 SERVINGS

SOUTHERN GRAVY POTATO BAKE

2 large sweet onion, chopped	2 tablespoons beef soup base, parve
1 tablespoon vegetable oil	¼ teaspoon garlic powder
4 tablespoons margarine	1 tablespoon soy sauce
¼ cup all-purpose flour	5-6 baking potatoes, peeled and sliced into ¼-inch thick slices
3 cups water	

Sauté onions in oil until tender and browned. Set aside. Melt margarine in a saucepan. Whisk in flour and cook until browned. Stir in water until smooth and thickened. Add soup base, garlic powder and soy sauce. Cook until smooth and thickened. Pour enough sauce to cover the bottom of a greased 13 x 9 x 2-inch baking dish. Layer potatoes on top. Spread onions over potatoes. Pour remaining sauce over all. Bake, covered, at 375 degrees for 30 minutes. Remove foil and bake an additional 30 minutes.

YIELD: 8 TO 10 SERVINGS

Brown bread crumbs in 3 tablespoon margarine and place on top for a crumb topping.

SOUTHWESTERN POTATO CASSEROLE

A South-of-the-border twist on traditional potato casserole!

2 packages potato pancake mix	2 (15 ounce) cans black beans, drained
4 eggs	1 (8 ounce) package shredded Cheddar cheese, divided
4½ cups water	
2 teaspoons chili powder	2 teaspoons plus 1 tablespoon vegetable oil, divided
1 (16 ounce) can diced green chilies, drained	Salt and pepper to taste
1 (16 ounce) can cream-style corn	

Combine potato pancake mix with eggs and water. Add chili powder, chilies, corn, black beans, and 1¼ cups Cheddar cheese. Grease bottom of baking dish with 2 teaspoons oil. Pour mixture into dish. Drizzle 1 tablespoon oil on top. Sprinkle with salt and pepper. Bake at 425 degrees for 30 minutes. Sprinkle with ¾ cup Cheddar cheese. Bake an additional 15 minutes.

YIELD: 8 TO 10 SERVINGS

ROASTED POTATOES

*An agronomist in the 1700s convinced the common French people
that potatoes were safe to eat by using reverse psychology. He posted guards
around his potato fields by day, by night he left the fields unguarded. Every
night, thieves would sneak into his fields and steal sacks of potatoes.*

2 **pounds red potatoes, quartered or smaller**	2 **teaspoons salt**
2 **onion, sliced into rings**	½ **teaspoon pepper**
⅓ **cup olive oil**	3 **garlic cloves, minced**
	2 **tablespoons paprika**

Boil potatoes for 20 minutes. Drain and place in a 13 x 9 x 2-inch baking dish. Layer onion over potatoes. Blend oil, salt, pepper, garlic, and paprika. Pour over potatoes. Bake at 375 degrees for 1 hour, 15 minutes. May assemble and refrigerate until ready to bake.

YIELD: 8 TO 10 SERVINGS

POTATOES AND ARTICHOKES

*A marinade of capers and artichokes impart
a subtle tang to the golden browned potatoes.*

6-8 Yukon gold potatoes, sliced
1 medium onion, coarsely chopped
2 tablespoons capers
2 (6 ounce) jars marinated artichoke
   hearts

2 tablespoons olive oil
   Seasoned salt and coarsely
    ground pepper
2 tablespoons chopped parsley

Preheat oven to 400 degrees. Scatter potato and onion in a greased 13 x 9 x 2-inch baking dish. Top with capers and artichoke with marinade. Drizzle with oil. Sprinkle with salt and pepper. Bake at 400 degrees for 30 minutes. Top with parsley. Reduce heat to 300 degrees. Cover and bake for 1 hour, 30 minutes.

YIELD: 10 TO 12 SERVINGS

BROTHER'S FAVORITE SPINACH

*A versatile dish that also makes a wonderful dip with crackers! No one remembers who
"brother" is although this recipe has been in one Memphis family for generations!*

2 (10 ounce) packages frozen
   chopped spinach, thawed
½ cup finely chopped onions
1 stick butter

1 (14 ounce) can artichokes, drained
   and chopped
1 (16 ounce) container sour cream
½ cup Parmesan cheese, divided
   Salt and pepper to taste

Cook spinach according to package directions. Drain well. Sauté onion in butter until slightly browned. Combine spinach, onion, artichokes, sour cream, ¼ cup Parmesan cheese, salt, and pepper. Spoon mixture into a buttered casserole dish. Top with remaining Parmesan cheese. Bake at 350 degrees for 20-30 minutes.

YIELD: 6 TO 8 SERVINGS

AUTUMN APPLE SQUASH BAKE

*A perfect casserole for the Rosh Hashanah meal, but easy
enough to accompany a nice weekday supper. It has all the flavors of fall!*

TOPPING
2 cups graham cracker crumbs	2 tablespoons margarine, softened
½ cup packed brown sugar	½ cup crushed nuts

TOPPING

Combine cracker crumbs, brown sugar, margarine, and nuts. Set aside.

SQUASH
1 large butternut squash	1 tablespoon brown sugar
5½ tablespoons margarine, softened and divided	Pinch of white pepper
¼ teaspoon salt	2 pounds apples, peeled and sliced
	¼ cup sugar

SQUASH

Cut squash in half and scoop out seeds. Bake at 350 degrees for 30 minutes, cut side down. Scoop out pulp and mash. Add 4 tablespoons margarine, salt, brown sugar, and pepper. Melt 1½ tablespoons margarine in a skillet. Add apples and sugar. Cover and simmer until tender. Spoon apple mixture into a 13 x 9 x 2-inch baking dish. Spread squash evenly over apples. Sprinkle with topping. Bake at 350 degrees for 30 minutes.

YIELD: 10 TO 12 SERVINGS

ZUCCHINI WITH BASIL AND ALMONDS

Summery Southern zucchini dressed in a nutty, fragrant marinade.

¼ cup olive oil, divided	1 tablespoon lemon juice
6 zucchini, cut into ¼-inch slices	¼ teaspoon red pepper
¼ cup slivered almonds, toasted	Salt and pepper to taste
¼ cup chopped basil	

Heat 1 tablespoon oil in a large skillet. Sauté zucchini about 5-10 minutes until tender and slightly browned. Remove from skillet. Add 3 tablespoons oil to skillet. Stir in almonds, basil, lemon juice, red pepper, salt, and pepper. Cook until thoroughly heated. Return zucchini and toss to coat.

YIELD: 8 TO 10 SERVINGS

ZUCCHINI CARROT TERRINE

A Southern twist on an Eastern European classic.

CARROT

2	carrots, peeled	1	teaspoon salt
1	potato, peeled	½	teaspoon baking powder
1	onion	1½	cups all-purpose flour
2	tablespoons ketchup		Dash of pepper
½	cup vegetable oil		

CARROT

Combine carrot, potato, onion, ketchup, oil, salt, baking powder, flour, and pepper in a food processor. Process until smooth. Pour mixture into a greased 13 x 9 x 2-inch baking dish. Bake at 350 degrees for 30 minutes.

ZUCCHINI

1	onion, chopped	1½	pounds zucchini, unpeeled and sliced into thin rounds
1	(4 ounce) package mushrooms, sliced		

ZUCCHINI

Sauté onion, mushrooms, and zucchini in a skillet. Drain liquid and transfer to a bowl.

TOPPING

2	eggs	¼	teaspoon pepper
¼	cup matzo meal	2	tablespoons mayonnaise (optional)
¼	teaspoon salt		

TOPPING

Blend eggs, matzo meal, salt, pepper, and mayonnaise until smooth. Add to zucchini mixture. Mix well. Spoon over carrot layer. Bake at 350 degrees for 45 minutes-1 hour until slightly browned.

YIELD: 10 TO 12 SERVINGS

Don't let the idea of a terrine intimidate you — this dish is relatively easy to put together and the presentation is worth it!

TOMATOES ROCKEFELLER

Always a crowd pleaser on the buffet table and versatile enough for brunch or dinner.

2 (10 ounce) packages frozen chopped spinach, thawed
1 cup seasoned bread crumbs
6 eggs, slightly beaten
½ teaspoon minced garlic
½ teaspoon pepper
1 teaspoon Tabasco sauce
6 green onions, chopped
1½ sticks margarine, melted
¼ teaspoon Worcestershire sauce
1 teaspoon salt
1 teaspoon dried thyme
12 thick slices tomato

Cook spinach according to package directions. Drain well. Combine spinach, bread crumbs, eggs, garlic, pepper, Tabasco, green onion, margarine, Worcestershire sauce, salt, and thyme. Mix well. Arrange tomatoes in a single layer in a greased 13 x 9 x 2-inch baking dish. Spread spinach mixture over tomatoes. Bake at 350 degrees for 15 minutes.

YIELD: 10 TO 12 SERVINGS

Topping freezes well or may be spread thinner to cover more tomatoes.

Desserts

To Essie, our Mom and our Mimi,

You are a gracious hostess whose Sabbath tables are always exquisitely set.

We love you and appreciate the special touch you add to our lives.

Mike and the family

Raised in Memphis, Evelyn Graber acquired an appreciation for everything sweet at an early age. Her Russian mother not only fostered a love of sweets and desserts in her daughter, but also taught her how to prepare those delicacies. Although Evelyn consumed her fair share of chicken fat as a child, she quickly amended her mother's recipes, substituting heart healthy ingredients for *schmaltz* and fat. Today, her recipes defy the stereotypes about both Southern and Jewish food. Evelyn certainly proves that great entertaining can be delicious and good for you!

LEMON MERINGUE PIE

*Be sure the meringue touches the crust around the entire edge with
no openings to make a dry seal. The hot filling will cook the meringue's bottom
first, which also helps seal the edges as the meringue browns.*

1½ **cups sugar**	5 **tablespoons margarine**
3 **tablespoons cornstarch**	**Zest of ½ lemon**
3 **tablespoons all-purpose flour**	⅓ **cup plus 1 tablespoon lemon juice**
Dash of salt	2 **(9 inch) baked pie shells, deep**
1½ **cups hot water**	**dish**
4 **slightly beaten egg yolks**	**Meringue**

In a saucepan, mix first 4 ingredients; gradually add hot water (from Instant Hot is fine), stirring constantly. Cook and stir over medium-high heat until mixture comes to a boil. Reduce heat; cook and stir 2 minutes longer. Remove from heat.

Stir a moderate amount of hot mixture into egg yolks, then add egg mixture to hot mixture. Bring to boiling and cook 2 minutes, stirring constantly. Add margarine and lemon zest. Slowly add lemon juice, mixing well. Pour into pastry shell. Spread meringue over filling; seal to edge of shell. Bake at 325 degrees for 30 minutes.

MERINGUE

1 **tablespoon cornstarch**
2 **tablespoons sugar**
½ **cup water**
7 **egg whites**
Dash of salt
¾ **cup sugar**
2 **teaspoons vanilla**

Cook cornstarch, sugar, and water until thick. Set aside.

Beat 7 egg whites and dash of salt until peaks form. Add prepared cornstarch mixture 1 tablespoon at a time. Beat until creamy. Add ¾ cup sugar and 2 teaspoons vanilla until sugar dissolves. Spread on filling.

CHOCOLATE CHESS PIE

Chess pie is one of the South's great contributions to the culinary arts.
One folk story asserts that it was originally called "just pie," which was drawled as
"jus' pie," eventually rolling off the tongue as "chess pie." This is always a favorite!

1¼ cups sugar
¼ cup unsweetened cocoa powder
4 tablespoons margarine, melted
2 eggs
10 tablespoons soymilk
1½ teaspoons vanilla

⅛ teaspoon salt
1 (9-inch) pie shell, unbaked
1 (8 ounce) container frozen
   whipped topping, thawed
Chocolate syrup

Preheat oven to 350 degrees. Combine sugar, cocoa, and margarine in a bowl. Add eggs and beat until smooth. Blend in soymilk, vanilla, and salt. Pour filling into pie shell. Bake at 350 degrees for 45 minutes until tester comes out clean. Cool. Top with whipped topping. Pie freezes well. Drizzle chocolate syrup across the top!

YIELD: 8 SERVINGS

CORKY'S FUDGE PIE

This classic tops the list of many Memphian's cravings.

2 cups sugar
½ cup all-purpose flour
½ cup cocoa powder
2 sticks margarine, melted

4 eggs
½ teaspoon vanilla
½ cup chopped pecans

Preheat oven to 375 degrees. Sift together sugar, flour, and cocoa. Stir in margarine until smooth. Add eggs and vanilla. Beat with a mixer on low speed until just combined, do not over beat. Stir in pecans. Pour filling into a greased and floured 10-inch pie pan. Bake at 375 degrees for 20-30 minutes. Serve warm.

YIELD: 10 SERVINGS

CLASSIC PECAN PIE

"Pecan" comes from the Indian name "pecane" which means "nut to be cracked with a rock." The French created pecan pie after settling in New Orleans.

1	cup corn syrup
¾	cup sugar
¼	teaspoon salt
1	teaspoon vanilla
2	teaspoons lemon juice
4	tablespoons margarine, melted
3	eggs
1	cup crushed pecans
1	(9-inch) pie shell, unbaked

Preheat oven to 350 degrees. Combine corn syrup, sugar, salt, vanilla, lemon juice, and margarine. Stir in eggs and pecans until smooth. Pour filling into pie shell. Bake at 350 degrees for 1 hour.

YIELD: 8 SERVINGS

PUMPKIN PIE

1	deep dish pie shell	½	teaspoon cinnamon
4	eggs, lightly beaten	¼	teaspoon ginger
2	cups canned pumpkin	¼	teaspoon nutmeg
1	cup sugar	¼	teaspoon allspice
½	cup light corn syrup	¼	teaspoon salt
1	teaspoon vanilla		

Bake pie shell at 350 degrees for 5 minutes. Combine all other ingredients and pumpkin into shell. Bake 50-60 minutes or until filling is set.

SPLENDID APPLE PIE

Double crust pie pastry, divided
7 cups peeled baking apple slices
1 cup sugar substitute
3 tablespoons cornstarch

¾ teaspoon cinnamon
¼ teaspoon ground nutmeg
⅛ teaspoon salt

Preheat oven to 425 degrees. Press one pastry sheet in pie plate. Bake pastry a few minutes until lightly browned. Remove from oven.

Place apples in a large bowl. Combine sugar substitute, cornstarch, cinnamon, nutmeg, and salt in a small bowl. Sprinkle mixture over apples and toss to coat. Spoon mixture into pie shell. Place second pastry sheet over filling, sealing edges to bottom pastry. Cut small slits in top of pastry. Bake at 425 degrees for 40-50 minutes or until golden browned. Serve warm or cold.

YIELD: 8 TO 10 SERVINGS

Place pie plate on a baking sheet to catch any filling that bubbles over. May also combine ½ cup blueberries with apple mixture for variation.

FIGURE WATCHIN' FUDGE PIE

½ cup sugar substitute
½ cup cocoa powder
⅓ cup all-purpose flour
2 egg yolks
2 cups milk or soymilk

2 tablespoons margarine
1 teaspoon vanilla
1 (9-inch) pie shell, baked
   Whipped cream and crushed
     sugar-free chocolate cookies for
     garnish

Combine sugar substitute, cocoa, and flour in a saucepan. Stir in egg yolks, milk, margarine, and vanilla. Cook over medium heat until thickened, stirring constantly to avoid burning or lumps. Pour filling into pie shell. Refrigerate. Top with whipped cream and cookies crumbs.

YIELD: 8 SERVINGS

RAW APPLE CINNAMON CAKE

1½ cups vegetable oil
2 cups sugar
2 eggs
3 cups all-purpose flour
1 teaspoon baking soda
½ teaspoon salt

2 teaspoons cinnamon
2 teaspoons vanilla
3 cups chopped apples, peeled and
     cored
1 cup chopped pecans
   Powdered sugar

Combine oil, sugar, and eggs until smooth. Sift together flour, baking soda, salt, and cinnamon. Add to creamed mixture. Mix well. Stir in vanilla, apples, and pecans. Pour batter into a greased and lightly floured Bundt pan. Bake at 350 degrees for 1 hour, 30 minutes. Cool 15 minutes in pan. Remove from pan and cool completely. Dust cooled cake with powdered sugar.

YIELD: 12 TO 15 SERVINGS

RED VELVET CAKE

Do not substitute any ingredients!

2 (1 ounce) bottles red food coloring	2 eggs
3 tablespoons cocoa	1 cup buttermilk
1½ cups sugar	1 teaspoon vanilla
2¼ cups cake flour	1 teaspoon almond extract
¼ teaspoon salt	1 tablespoon vinegar
½ cup shortening	1 teaspoon baking soda

Mix food coloring and cocoa together to make a paste. Set aside. Sift sugar, flour, and salt. Beat shortening and eggs until blended. Be sure to cream thoroughly adding alternating dry ingredients with buttermilk. After adding the dry ingredients and buttermilk, then add food coloring paste. Add vanilla and almond extracts to mixture.

In a small bowl, mix vinegar and baking soda by hand. Add to buttermilk mixture and stir. Pour into 2 round or square greased and floured cake pans. Bake at 350 degrees for 30-40 minutes.

ICING

4½ tablespoons flour	1 cup sugar
1 cup milk	1 teaspoon vanilla
½ pound butter (not margarine)	

Combine milk in flour stirring to keep from lumping. Cover over low heat stirring occasionally until thick; set aside to cool. Cream butter, beating 4 minutes. Add sugar and beat 4 minutes more. Add flour paste and vanilla and beat 4 minutes more (important). Do not beat less than 12 minutes. Frost cake afer cake has cooled.

CHEESECAKE

Cheesecake was served in 776 BCE to the athletes in the first Olympic Games.

CRUST

⅓ (13½ ounce) package graham cracker crumbs

6 tablespoons butter, melted

CRUST

Combine cracker crumbs and butter. Press into bottom and up sides of 9-inch springform pan.

FILLING

3 (8 ounce) packages cream cheese, softened

1 cup sugar

4 eggs

1 teaspoon vanilla

Dash of salt

1 tablespoon all-purpose flour

FILLING

Beat cream cheese, sugar, eggs, vanilla, salt, and flour with a mixer 20 minutes until smooth. Pour over crust. Bake at 325 degrees for 45 minutes.

TOPPING

1 pint sour cream

⅓ cup sugar

1 teaspoon vanilla

TOPPING

Blend sour cream, sugar and vanilla. Spread over filling. Bake at 325 degrees for 10 minutes. Refrigerate overnight.

YIELD: 16 SERVINGS

Desserts

BLACK HAT

The name comes from this dessert's appearance
when it is inverted from the ramekins.

3 sticks plus 4 tablespoons margarine
2¼ cups chopped bittersweet chocolate
2½ cups powdered sugar
6 egg yolks
7 whole eggs
1¼ cups all-purpose flour

Melt margarine and chocolate in top of a double boiler over simmering water. Blend powdered sugar, egg yolks, eggs, and flour with a mixer. Add chocolate mixture and mix well. Divide batter among 4-ounce greased ramekins until three-fourths full. Bake at 350 degrees for 8-10 minutes.

YIELD: 12 SERVINGS

CHOCOLATE CHIP CAKE

1 (18 ounce) package yellow cake mix
1 (3 ounce) package instant vanilla pudding mix
1 (8 ounce) container sour cream or parve sour cream
½ cup vegetable oil
½ cup water
4 eggs
1 (6 ounce) package mini semi-sweet chocolate chips
3 tablespoons sugar
3 tablespoons cocoa powder

Beat together cake mix, pudding mix, sour cream, oil, water, and eggs for 5-10 minutes. In a separate bowl, combine chocolate chips, sugar, and cocoa. Pour a layer of batter into a greased and lightly floured Bundt pan. Top with a layer of chocolate chip mixture. Repeat layers until gone. Bake at 350 degrees for 1 hour, 15 minutes.

YIELD: 15 SERVINGS

THREE DAY COCONUT CAKE

*The most important thing to know about
this recipe is that it does not take 3 days to make!*

1   (18 ounce) package butter cake
    mix
1¾ cups sugar
1   (16 ounce) container sour cream
    or parve sour cream

1   (12 ounce) package flaked coconut
1   (8 ounce) container frozen
    whipped topping, thawed

Prepare cake mix according to package directions, making two 8 or 9-inch cake layers. Cool completely. Combine sugar, sour cream, and coconut. Refrigerate coconut mixture. Slice each cake layer in half. Reserve 1 cup coconut mixture. Spread remaining coconut mixture between cake layers making a 4 layer high cake. Blend reserved coconut mixture with whipped topping until smooth. Spread mixture on top and sides of cake. Seal in an airtight container and refrigerate for **3** days before serving.

YIELD: 12 SERVINGS

14 KARAT CAKE

CAKE

4 eggs
1½ cups oil
2 cups sugar
2 cups grated raw carrots
1 (8 ounce) can pineapple, undrained
1 cup pecans
½ cup raisins

1 cup coconut
2 cups flour
2 teaspoons baking powder
1½ teaspoons baking soda
1 teaspoon salt
2 teaspoons cinnamon
½ teaspoon ground ginger

CAKE

Beat eggs slightly until smooth. Add oil and sugar. Mix well. Add carrots, pineapple, pecans, raisins, and coconut. Mix until all ingredients are moistened. Sift together flour, baking powder, baking soda, salt, cinnamon, and ground ginger. Add this dry mixture to the other ingredients. Pour into greased and floured cake pan, 3 (9-inch) layer pans or a deep 9 x 13-inch pan. Make sure oven rack is well above heat source in the oven so that the cake will not burn. Bake at 350 degrees for 35-40 minutes until cake springs back in the middle.

FROSTING

½ cup butter
1 (8 ounce) package cream cheese
1 teaspoon vanilla
1 pound powdered sugar

FROSTING

Cream butter and cream cheese together. When smooth add vanilla and mix well. Add sugar slowly and mix well after each addition. If mixture turns out a little thick add 1 teaspoon milk. Frost cake after cake has cooled.

HUMMINGBIRD CAKE

Food historians generally cite Mrs. L.H. Wiggins' recipe published in the February 1978 issue of Southern Living magazine as the first printed reference to "Hummingbird Cake." Mrs. Wiggins did not offer an explanation for the name.

CAKE

3 cups all-purpose flour	3 eggs
2 cups sugar	1½ teaspoons vanilla
1 teaspoon baking soda	1 (8 ounce) can crushed pineapple, drained
1 teaspoon salt	2 cups chopped bananas
1 teaspoon cinnamon	2 cups pecans
1½ cups vegetable oil	

CAKE

Sift together flour, sugar, baking soda, salt, and cinnamon in a large bowl. Add oil, eggs, vanilla, pineapple, bananas, and pecans. Mix well. Do not beat. Pour batter into a greased and floured 10-inch tube pan or 2 loaf pans. Bake at 350 degrees about 1 hour or until tester comes out clean.

ICING

1 (8 ounce) package cream cheese	1 pound powdered sugar
½ cup margarine, softened	2 teaspoons vanilla

ICING

Place cream cheese and margarine in a large mixing bowl and beat at low speed gradually adding the sugar. Increase speed to medium-high and beat for 4 minutes. Add vanilla.

YIELD: 15 SERVINGS

TROPICAL SHERBET

Mangoes account for about 50% of all tropical fruits produced worldwide. Ripe mangoes are bright colored, soft and have a sweet scent. To ripen mangoes, keep them at room temperature open to air. Ripe mangoes can be stored in the refrigerator for up to a week.

1 large mango, diced	1 cup water
1 (15 ounce) can cream of coconut	5 tablespoons lime juice

Combine mango and cream of coconut in a blender. Purée until smooth. Add water and lime juice. Refrigerate until chilled. Freeze, stirring every hour until hard.

YIELD: 4 SERVINGS

MUD ISLAND CHOCOLATE CHEESECAKE

A melt-in-your-mouth confection loaded with chocolate scrumptiousness!

CRUST

2	cups crushed chocolate wafer cookies	¼	cup sugar
		5	tablespoons butter, melted

CRUST

Combine cracker crumbs, sugar, and butter. Mix well. Press mixture into bottom and 2 inches up sides of a 9-inch springform pan. Freeze crust.

CHOCOLATE LAYER

1	(8 ounce) package cream cheese, softened	¼	teaspoon vanilla
¼	cup sugar	2	(10 ounce) squares semi-sweet chocolate, melted
1	egg	⅓	cup sour cream

CHOCOLATE LAYER

Beat cream cheese and sugar until fluffy. Blend in egg and vanilla. Stir in chocolate and sour cream. Spoon mixture over crust.

PECAN LAYER

1	(8 ounce) package cream cheese, softened	1	egg
⅓	cup packed brown sugar	½	teaspoon vanilla
1	tablespoon all-purpose flour	¼	cup chopped pecans

PECAN LAYER

Beat cream cheese, brown sugar, and flour until fluffy. Blend in egg and vanilla. Stir in pecans. Gently spoon mixture over chocolate layer.

SOUR CREAM LAYER

5	ounces cream cheese, softened	1	cup sour cream
¼	cup sugar	¼	teaspoon vanilla
1	egg	¼	teaspoon almond extract

SOUR CREAM LAYER

Beat cream cheese and sugar until fluffy. Blend in egg. Stir in sour cream, vanilla, and almond extract. Gently spoon over pecan layer. Bake at 325 degrees for 1 hour. Turn off oven and leave cheesecake in oven for 30 minutes with door ajar. Slide knife around edge of pan. Leave cheesecake in oven an additional 30 minutes. Cool on rack. Refrigerate for 8 hours. Remove from pan.

CHOCOLATE GLAZE

6	(1 ounce) squares semi-sweet chocolate	¾	cup sifted powdered sugar
4	tablespoons butter	2	tablespoons water
		1	teaspoon vanilla

CHOCOLATE GLAZE

Melt chocolate and butter in top of double boiler. Remove from heat. Stir in powdered sugar, water, and vanilla until smooth. Spread glaze over warm cheesecake.

YIELD: 16 SERVINGS

TOFU CHEESECAKE

2	cups graham cracker crumbs		Tofu sour cream
1	stick margarine, melted	1¼	cups sugar
4	(8 ounce) packages tofu cream cheese	1½-2	teaspoons vanilla
1½	cups sugar		
1½	tablespoons lemon juice or lime juice		
	Pinch of salt		
4	eggs		

Combine cracker crumbs and margarine. Press into bottom of 9-inch springform pan. Beat cream cheese, sugar, lemon juice, salt, and eggs with a mixer on high speed until fluffy. Pour mixture over crust. Bake at 325 degrees for 50-60 minutes or until lightly browned. Cool for 10 minutes. Blend sour cream, sugar, and vanilla. Spread over cooled cream cheese layer. Return to oven for 10 minutes. Do not over bake. Refrigerate immediately.

YIELD: 16 SERVINGS

Desserts

PEPPERMINT CHEESECAKE

1¼ cups chocolate cookie crumbs	1 (14 ounce) can condensed milk
¼ cup sugar	1 cup crushed hard peppermint candy
¼ cup butter	2 cups whipping cream, whipped
1 (8 ounce) package cream cheese, softened	

Combine crumbs, sugar and butter. Press on the bottom and halfway up sides of a 9-inch springform pan. Beat cream cheese until fluffy. Gradually beat in condensed milk, stir in crushed candy. Fold in whipped cream. Pour into pan. Cover and freeze until firm.

Sometimes you taste something so refreshing, so singular and so extraordinary that you remember the flavor months after your first bite. "Peppermint Cheesecake" was the first recipe we taste tested and it has withstood the test of time. Months later our mouths are still tingling from the unique taste of this scrumptious cheesecake.

BUTTERMILK POUND CAKE

1 cup shortening	3 cups flour (sifted once and then again with ½ teaspoon salt)
2 cups sugar, divided	¼ teaspoon baking soda
1 cup egg whites	1 cup buttermilk
6 eggs, separated	2 teaspoons vanilla in the milk

Cream shortening and 1 cup sugar, beat until fluffy. Add egg yolks one at a time. Add dry ingredients and buttermilk. In a separate mixing bowl, beat egg whites until stiff, gradually add remaining 1 cup of sugar. Fold the egg whites into the flour mixture. Grease and flour baking pans. Bake in 1 large loaf pan. Bake at 350 degrees for 1 hour. Cake is done when top is cracked.

Desserts

208

CHOCOLATE FUDGE CAKE

CAKE

2	cups all-purpose flour	2	eggs
2	cups sugar	½	buttermilk or ½ cup soymilk with ½ tablespoon vinegar
½	teaspoon salt	1	teaspoon baking soda
1¾	sticks margarine	1	teaspoon vanilla
1	cup water		
3	tablespoons cocoa powder		

CAKE

Sift flour. Measure flour again into sifter with sugar and salt and sift a second time into a bowl. Heat margarine, water, and cocoa until smooth. Remove from heat and cool.

In a separate bowl, beat eggs, buttermilk, baking soda, and vanilla. Set aside. Slowly add chocolate mixture to flour mixture. Mix well. Stir in milk mixture until smooth. Pour batter into a greased 13 x 9 x 2-inch baking dish. Bake at 350 degrees for 40-50 minutes.

FUDGE TOPPING

3	tablespoons cocoa powder	3½	cups powdered sugar
6	tablespoons margarine	1	teaspoon vanilla
5	tablespoons soymilk	1	cup chopped pecans (optional)

FUDGE TOPPING

Heat cocoa, margarine, soymilk, powdered sugar, and vanilla in a saucepan. Cook and stir until thickened. Add pecans. Immediately pour over hot cake. Cool uncovered. Freezes great in cut squares or whole cake.

YIELD: 12 SERVINGS

RICKI'S LEMON POPPY SEED CAKE

2¼ cups cake flour

1⅛ cups white sugar

1 teaspoon salt

1½ tablespoons lemon zest

4½ tablespoons poppy seeds

1⅓ cups unsalted margarine, softened

5 eggs

TOPPING, OPTIONAL

¾ cup white sugar

¾ cup lemon juice

Preheat oven to 350 degrees. Grease and flour one 9 x 5-inch loaf pan.

Mix together the flour, 1 cup plus 2 tablespoons white sugar, and salt. Then mix in the lemon zest, poppy seeds, and margarine. Beat in the eggs, one at a time, beating well after each addition. Pour batter into the prepared pan.

Bake at 350 degrees for 1 hour, 15 minutes or until a toothpick inserted in the center comes out clean.

Optional topping: In a saucepan over low heat; cook ¾ cup white sugar and the lemon juice stirring until sugar is dissolved. Let cool to just warm or to room temperature.

Remove the cake from the oven and place the pan on a wire rack-place a cookie sheet underneath this rack. (Brush the top of the cake with the warm or room temperature syrup, allowing lots of the syrup to run down and soak into the sides and bottom of the cake.) Cool slightly in the pan before removing the cake to the wire rack to cool completely.

Note: freezes well

YUM YUM CAKE

The name says it all! Get creative with garnishes:
powdered sugar, nuts, or additional chocolate chips are great places to start!

2 sticks margarine, softened

2 cups sugar

4 eggs

2½ cups all-purpose flour

3 teaspoons baking powder

1½ teaspoons vanilla

1 cup orange juice

1 (12 ounce) package semi-sweet chocolate chips, chopped

Cream margarine and sugar. Add eggs, flour, baking powder, vanilla, orange juice, and chocolate chips. Pour batter into a greased 13 x 9 x 2-inch baking dish. Bake at 350 degrees for 40 minutes.

YIELD: 12 SERVINGS

BRUNCH CAKE

2	sticks unsalted butter	¼	teaspoon baking soda
½	teaspoon salt	3	cups flour
3	cups sugar	½	teaspoon almond extract
5	large eggs	1½	teaspons vanilla
¾	cup of liquid consisting of 2½ tablespoons sour cream and the rest should be milk	¼	cup sugar
		¼	cup water
		2	tablespoons real coffee

Beat butter and salt together. Pour in 3 cups sugar and beat for 20 minutes. Add eggs, one at a time. Add milk mixture and baking soda. Sift flour in and mix. Add almond and vanilla extracts and beat well. In a seperate bowl add ¼ cup sugar, water, and coffee. Alternate pouring the light mixture and the dark mixture 3 times to 2 loaf pans. Bake at 300 degrees for 25 minutes and then at 325 degrees for 1 hour.

THE GENERAL'S CHOCOLATE CHOCOLATE CAKE

1	(6 ounce) package chocolate chips (almost 1 cup)	¼	cup water
¾	cup chopped pecans	1	teaspoon vanilla
1	box chocolate cake mix	1	small box instant chocolate pudding
4	eggs	1	(8 ounce) container sour cream
½	cup vegetable oil		

Coat the chocolate chips and pecans in a tablespoon or so of cake mix. Mix remaining ingredients together — fold in chocolate chip and pecan mixture. Pour into a greased and floured tube pan and bake at 350 degrees for about 50 minutes. Cook for 15 minutes in the pan. Frost when cool.

FROSTING

1	box powdered sugar	3	squares baking chocolate, melted
¾	stick soft margarine	⅔	can evaporated milk

Mix all ingredients adding evaporated milk a little at a time until it is a "thick" spreading consistency.

MEMPHIS BLUESBERRY CRUMBLE PIE

*Blueberries are native only to North America. "Rabbiteye" blueberries
grow from the Carolinas to the Gulf Coast states; "Hillside" blueberries grow from
Appalachia to the piedmont of the Southeast. The blueberry is considered a "superfood"
because of its nutrient richness and antioxidant strength.*

4	cups fresh blueberries		1	(9 inch) pie crust
½	cup sugar		½	cup flour
3	tablespoons flour		½	cup brown sugar
¼-½	teaspoon cinnamon		5	tablespoons margarine
	Squirt of lemon juice			

Preheat oven to 375 degrees. Mix blueberries, sugar, flour, cinnamon, and lemon juice and pour into pie crust. Combine flour, brown sugar, and margarine until crumbly, set aside. Cover edges of pie crust with foil. Sprinkle crumble mixture on top of pie filling and bake for 25 minutes. Remove foil and continue to bake for 25-30 minutes.

BLACKBERRY COBBLER

*The University of Arkansas has developed several varieties of blackberries including
"Navajo," "Ouachita," "Cherokee," "Apache, " "Arapahoe," and "Kiowa."*

1⅓	cups sugar		2	(14 ounce) packages frozen blackberries, thawed
1	stick margarine, melted		1	frozen pie pastry, thawed
½	cup all-purpose flour		1	tablespoon sugar
2	teaspoons vanilla			

Combine sugar, margarine, flour, and vanilla. Add blackberries. Gently spoon mixture into a lightly greased 11 x 7 x 2-inch baking dish. Cut pie pastry into 1-inch wide strips. Arrange strips diagonally over fruit. Sprinkle with sugar. Bake at 425 degrees for 45 minutes or until golden browned. Serve with a scoop of parve ice cream or whipped topping.

YIELD: 8 TO 10 SERVINGS

Frozen blueberries are a good substitute!

Desserts

CHAMPION COBBLER FROM LOUISIANA PEACH FESTIVAL

The north Louisiana town of Ruston, located between
Monroe and Shreveport, is famous for its luscious peaches.

FILLING

8-9 peaches, peeled and sliced

½ cup water

1 cup sugar

2 tablespoons all-purpose flour

Pinch of salt

1 stick margarine, melted

FILLING

Cook peaches in water until tender. Combine sugar, flour, and salt in a bowl. Add peaches and margarine. Mix well.

PASTRY

2 cups all-purpose flour

1 teaspoon salt

⅔ cup vegetable shortening

⅓ cup soymilk

PASTRY

Blend flour, salt, and shortening until resembles coarse meal. Stir in soymilk. Refrigerate. Roll dough out on a floured board. Cut dough to fit in bottom of 13 x 9 x 2-inch baking dish. Pour peach filling over top. Cover with lattice strips of dough. Bake at 350 degrees for 40-45 minutes or until browned.

YIELD: 10 TO 12 SERVINGS

FRUIT PIZZA

A Southern spin on an Italian classic!

CRUST

1	stick margarine, softened	1	teaspoon baking powder
¾	cup sugar	½	teaspoon vanilla
1	egg	1½	cups all-purpose flour

CRUST

Combine margarine, sugar, and egg. Stir in baking powder, vanilla, and flour. Roll out dough to fit a greased pizza pan. Bake at 350 degrees for 15-20 minutes Cool.

FILLING

1	container heavy cream or parve whipping cream
1	(3 ounce) package instant vanilla pudding mix

Seasonal summer fruits-thinly sliced kiwi, strawberries, blackberries, blueberries, raspberries, or Mandarin oranges

FILLING

Beat cream and pudding mix with a mixer. Spread on top of crust. Arrange fruit over cream filling.

GLAZE

½	cup sugar	2	tablespoons lemon juice
1	tablespoon cornstarch	½	cup water
½	cup orange juice		

GLAZE

Heat sugar, cornstarch, orange juice, lemon juice, and water in a saucepan about 4 minutes until thickened. Cool. Spoon over fruit. Serve immediately.

YIELD: 8 TO 10 SERVINGS

FRUIT WITH CRUNCH

Think of these as sundaes without the ice cream!

TOPPING

1 cup chopped nuts	1 cup crispy rice cereal
½ cup packed brown sugar	4 tablespoons margarine, softened

CRUNCH TOPPING

Combine nuts, brown sugar, cereal, and margarine. Mix well. Spread onto a baking sheet. Bake at 350 degrees for 15 minutes. Cool and crumble.

FRUIT

4 oranges, sectioned	1 (10 ounce) package frozen raspberries, thawed
2 green apples, chopped	
2 red apples, chopped	½ cup orange juice
2 yellow apples, chopped	2 tablespoons powdered sugar
1 (10 ounce) package frozen strawberries, thawed	

FRUIT

Place oranges and all apples in a bowl. Combine strawberries, raspberries, orange juice, and powdered sugar in a blender. Process until smooth. Sprinkle half crunch topping over fruit. Drizzle with sauce and top with more crunch topping.

YIELD: 10 TO 12 SERVINGS

COOKIES N' CREAM ICE CREAM PIE

1 package sandwich cookies, crushed (reserve 2 tablespoons)	½ cup sugar
	2 teaspoons vanilla
2 containers whipped topping	1 tablespoon prepared coffee
4 eggs	

Line 1 deep dish pie plate or a springform pan with some crushed sandwich cookies to cover bottom. Whip all whipped topping, eggs, sugar, and vanilla together until stiff. Quickly fold into cookie crumbs. Sprinkle reserved 2 tablespoons crushed cookies on top. Freeze. Let thaw 15 minutes before serving.

VANILLA ICE CREAM

We love making Root Beer floats with the ice cream.
It is always a crowd pleaser for the kids and adults.

2   containers heavy cream or
      parve whipping cream
¾   cup sugar

6   eggs
3   teaspoons vanilla

Beat cream until thickened. Beat in sugar, eggs, and vanilla. Freeze.

YIELD: 6 TO 8 SERVINGS

For variations, add semi-sweet chocolate chips. Or add green food coloring, mint or peppermint extract, and chocolate chips for Mint Chocolate Chip flavor.

HOT FUDGE SAUCE

You won't find anything this good in a jar! This recipe comes from the files of a Memphis family that treasures it as a favorite. It stores well in the refrigerator.

1 stick butter
4 (1 ounce) squares
   unsweetened chocolate
2 cups sugar

1 (12 ounce) can evaporated
   milk
Dash of salt
2 teaspoons vanilla

Melt butter and chocolate in a saucepan. Stir in sugar and milk. Sprinkle salt on top. Cook for 20 minutes, stirring constantly. Bring to boil. Remove from heat and cool. Stir in vanilla.

YIELD: 2 CUPS

FROZEN BUTTER-FINGERS

GRAHAM CRACKER CRUST LAYER

1¼ cups whole graham crackers, crushed

½ stick margarine, melted

2 tablespoons sugar

Combine crust layer ingredients, reserving ¼ cup to sprinkle over top for topping. Press the rest into the bottom of 8 x 8-inch dish to form a crust.

CHOCOLATE LAYER

6 ounces semi-sweet chocolate chips

3 tablespoons oil

Melt together and put a thin layer over crust, reserving some to drizzle on top.

ICE CREAM

1 (8 ounce) container frozen whipped topping, thawed

½-¾ cup peanut butter

½ cup marshmallow fluff

2 tablespoons margarine, melted

Whip the whipped topping and add other ingredients. Spread over chocolate layer and crust. Drizzle remaining chocolate and sprinkle crumbs on top.

FREEZE! Pull out to defrost a little before serving.

RAINBOW SHERBET

2 cups water

2 cups sugar

2 (3 ounce) packages strawberry flavored gelatin

2 cups orange juice

2 cups pineapple juice

Combine water, sugar, and gelatin in a saucepan. Bring to boil. Reduce heat and simmer until thickened. Cool. Add orange juice and pineapple juice. Pour in a shallow pan. Freeze at least 6 hours. Break up and place in mixer bowl. Beat and pour into a container. Freeze.

YIELD: 8 SERVINGS

PIÑA COLADA SHERBET

*For a festive presentation, serve in a glass goblet and
garnish with a slice of pineapple and a cherry. Splash of rum is optional.*

1	(15 ounce) can cream of coconut	1	cup orange juice
1	(15 ounce) can crushed pineapple	¼	cup rum

Combine cream of coconut, pineapple, orange juice, and rum. Refrigerate until cold. Transfer to freezer until frozen. Break into pieces. Blend or process until fluffy. Return to freezer until firm.

YIELD: 4 SERVINGS

CHOCOLATE RASPBERRY BARS

2	sticks margarine, softened	1	cup semi-sweet chocolate chips
1½	cups sugar, divided	4	egg whites
2	egg yolks	¼	teaspoon salt
2½	cups all-purpose flour	2	cups finely chopped nuts
1	(10 ounce) jar apricot preserves or raspberry jelly		

Cream margarine, ½ cup sugar, and egg yolks. Add flour and knead with hands. Press mixture into bottom of a greased 13 x 9 x 2-inch baking dish. Bake at 350 degrees for 15-20 minutes or until lightly browned. Remove from oven. Spread preserves over crust. Top with chocolate chips. Beat egg whites and salt until stiff. Fold in 1 cup sugar and nuts. Spread over chocolate chips. Bake at 350 degrees about 25 minutes. Cut into 3 x 1-inch bars.

YIELD: 12 SERVINGS

MISSISSIPPI MUD BROWNIES

BROWNIES

1	cup chopped pecans	½	cup unsweetened cocoa powder
2	sticks butter or margarine	4	large eggs
1	(4 ounce) semi-sweet chocolate baking bar, chopped	1	teaspoon vanilla
2	cups sugar	¾	teaspoon salt
1½	cups all-purpose flour	1	(7 ounce) jar marshmallow fluff

BROWNIES

Preheat oven to 350 degrees. Place pecans in a single layer in a shallow pan. Bake 8-10 minutes until toasted and fragrant. Place butter or margarine and chocolate in a large glass bowl. Microwave on high power 1 minute, stirring at 30 seconds intervals or until smooth. Whisk in sugar, flour, cocoa, eggs, vanilla, and salt. Pour batter into a greased 15 x 10 x 1-inch jelly roll pan. Bake at 350 degrees for 20 minutes. Remove from oven and spread marshmallow fluff on top.

CHOCOLATE FROSTING

1	stick butter or margarine	1	(16 ounce) package powdered sugar
⅓	cup milk or soymilk		
¼	cup unsweetened cocoa powder	1	teaspoon vanilla

CHOCOLATE FROSTING

Melt butter or margarine in a saucepan. Whisk in milk and cocoa. Bring to boil, whisking constantly. Remove from heat. Gradually add powdered sugar, stirring until smooth. Stir in vanilla. Immediately drizzle frosting over warm brownies. Sprinkle with toasted pecans.

YIELD: 16 SERVINGS

AMBROSIA

2	cans pineapple chunks	1	jar marshallow cream
1	jar maraschino cherries, halved	1	small package coconut
2	small cans Mandarin oranges	1	small carton whipped topping
1	cup nuts		

Drain all fruits thoroughly. Mix and place in dish for serving. Mix in marshmallow cream. Add stiffly whipped cream by folding into other ingredients. Mix small amount of coconut through fruit mixture and top with layer of the rest of the coconut. Place a few cherries on top.

Desserts

219

OLD HENRY BARS

2   sticks butter or margarine, softened
1   cup firmly packed brown sugar
4   cups rolled oats

¾   cup chunky or creamy peanut butter
1   (12 ounce) package semi-sweet chocolate chips

Blend butter or margarine, brown sugar, and oats. Press mixture on a greased 15 x 10 x 2 inch jelly roll pan or on a 1-inch baking sheet. Bake at 350 degrees for 15 minutes. While warm, spread peanut butter over crust. Melt chocolate chips in the microwave. Spread over peanut butter. Cool in refrigerator. Cut into squares.

YIELD: 16 TO 20 SERVINGS

LEMON BARS

Lemonade reinvented as a brownie!

2¼ cups all-purpose flour, divided
½   cup powdered sugar
2   sticks margarine, softened
4   eggs

1   teaspoon baking powder
½   teaspoon salt
4-6 tablespoons lemon juice
2   cups sugar

Cream 2 cups flour, powdered sugar and margarine until smooth. Press mixture into bottom of a greased 13 x 9 x 2-inch baking dish. Bake at 325 degrees for 20 minutes. Do not brown. Blend eggs, ¼ cup flour, baking powder, salt, lemon juice, and sugar. Pour mixture over crust. Bake at 325 degrees for 30 minutes. Sprinkle with powdered sugar. Immediately cut into squares.

YIELD: 15 SERVINGS

Desserts

HOWDY DOLLIES

A classic favorite that never fails to get raves!

1¾ cups graham cracker crumbs	1 cup semi-sweet chocolate chips
¼ cup sugar	1 cup chopped nuts
1 stick butter, softened	1 (14 ounce) can sweetened condensed milk
1 cup grated coconut	

Combine cracker crumbs, sugar, and butter. Press into bottom of 13 x 9 x 2-inch baking dish. Sprinkle with coconut, chocolate chips, and nuts. Pour milk over top. Bake at 350 degrees for 30-35 minutes. Cool and cut into squares.

YIELD: 15 SERVINGS

ORANGE-PECAN SHORTBREAD

Let's clear up the confusion: Shortcake is a sweet biscuit that is typically crumbly and moist. Shortbread is a traditional Scottish cookie known for its buttery taste. In this recipe, the dough log may be frozen for up to 3 months.

1 stick unsalted margarine, softened	¼ teaspoon salt
¼ cup powdered sugar	2 teaspoons grated orange zest
1 cup minus 1 tablespoon all-purpose flour	¾ cup chopped pecans
	Powdered sugar for garnish

Cream margarine and powdered sugar with an electric mixer. Beat on high speed for 2 minutes until light and creamy. Gradually beat in flour, salt, and orange zest. Shape dough into an 8-inch log. Place pecans on a sheet of plastic wrap. Roll log onto pecans to coat. Wrap log in plastic wrap and refrigerate for 2 hours.

Preheat oven to 300 degrees. Cut log into ½-inch slices. Place on an ungreased baking sheet. Bake at 300 degrees for 25-30 minutes. Cool on wire rack. Dust with powdered sugar.

YIELD: 16 COOKIES

THUMBPRINT COOKIES

Thumbprint cookies are also called "Polish tea cakes."
Experiment to find your own favorite fillings. The great thing about these
cookies is they are made without processed sugar, eggs, or white flour.

2	sticks margarine	2	cups flour plus 2 tablespoons all-purpose flour
¼	cup sugar		
¼	tespoon salt	½	cup finely ground pecans
2	teaspoons vanilla		

In a bowl let margarine come to room temperature. Add sugar and combine together with a spoon. Add salt, vanillla and gradually add the flour — a little at a time. Make sure to incorparate as you keep adding. Add the pecans and work the dough with your hands. If it is sticky add just a little more flour. Form the dough into a very small mound and make your little finger indention in the middle. Each cookie is free form and should be small (about ½ teaspoon size). Place on a cookie sheet lined with parchment paper. Bake at 350 degrees for 13-15 minutes. You want the cookie to be slightly brown. Cool completely before icing.

ICING

1¼ cups powdered sugar	1½ tablespoons water
¼ teasoon almond extract	Food coloring — your choice

ICING

In a bowl mix powdered sugar, almond extract, and water. It should be slightly thick. You can divide the icing into 2-3 bowls and add a few drops of different food coloring to each bowl. Get it to a color you like. Add just a little of icing to the middle of each cookie. Switch off the colors, and when you plate them, they will look beautiful.

CHOCOLATE SORBET

¾	cup sugar	2	cups hot water
¾	cup cocoa powder	½	teaspoon vanilla

Combine sugar and cocoa. Slowly whisk in hot water until smooth. Stir in vanilla. Freeze. Run through food processor and refreeze.

YIELD: 2 SERVINGS

PRALINE BARS

Graham crackers
1 cup packed light brown sugar

2 sticks butter or margarine
1 cup chopped pecans

Preheat oven to 350 degrees. Break graham crackers into 4 sections. Line baking sheet with crackers, about 52 crackers. Combine brown sugar and butter or margarine in a saucepan. Bring to boil, stirring constantly. Boil for 2 minutes. Stir in pecans. Pour over graham crackers. Bake at 350 degrees for 8-10 minutes. Cool in pan. Store in an airtight container for up to 10 days. This freezes well.

YIELD: 20 SERVINGS

PEANUT BUTTER JELLY BARS

2½ cups all-purpose flour
½ teaspoon baking powder
2 sticks (1 cup) salted butter or margarine
1 cup sugar

1 large egg
2 teaspoons vanilla extract
¾ cup jam or jelly
½ cup creamy peanut butter
2 tablespoons powdered sugar

Preheat oven to 350 degrees. Lightly coat a 13 x 9-inch baking pan with cooking spray. Set aside. In a medium bowl, sift together flour and baking powder. Set aside. In a large bowl, with electric mixer, combine butter or margarine and sugar. Add egg and vanilla extract and mix until smooth. Add flour mixture and blend at low speed until thoroughly combined. Divide dough into 2 pieces. Form disks and wrap tightly with plastic wrap. Refrigerate for 1 hour. Press one portion of dough into pan so that it is up ¾-inch on sides. Refrigerate 10 minutes. Spread half of jelly on dough. Layer peanut butter on top, then remaining jelly. Sprinkle with powdered sugar. Take second portion of dough and divide into small batches. Press each batch flat and put on top of peanut butter and jelly layer so that it forms a single piece on top (the dough will be sticky). Bake 35-40 minutes or until golden brown and firm to the touch in the center. Cool in pan and cut into squares.

YIELD: 24 SQUARES

CRANBERRY BISCOTTI

The word biscotti is derived from the Italian words
"bis" meaning twice and "cotto" meaning "baked."

- 2½ cups all-purpose flour
- 1 teaspoon baking powder
- ½ teaspoon salt
- 1½ cups sugar
- 1 stick margarine, softened
- 2 eggs

- ½ teaspoon almond extract
- 1½ cups dried cranberries
- 1 egg white
- 4 ounces white chocolate, melted (optional)

Combine flour, baking powder, and salt. Cream sugar, margarine, eggs, and almond extract with a mixer. Beat flour mixture into creamed mixture. Stir in cranberries. Divide dough in half. Refrigerate until cold.

Preheat oven to 350 degrees. Using floured hands, shape chilled dough into 10 x 2½-inch logs. Place on a greased baking sheet. Whisk egg white and brush on top and sides of each log. Bake at 350 degrees for 35 minutes or until golden brown. Cut into slices. Place each piece on its side. Bake an additional 5 minutes. Turn each piece and bake another 5 minutes. Cool. Melt chocolate and drizzle on biscotti. Let stand until set.

YIELD: 12 SERVINGS

GRASSHOPPER PIE

- 1½ cups cold milk
- ¼ teaspoon peppermint extract
- 1 package pistachio flavor instant pudding

- 2 cups thawed whipped topping
- 1 square semi-sweet chocolate, chopped
- 1 prepared chocolate wafer crust

Beat milk, extract, and pudding mix with whisk for 2 minutes. Stir in whipped topping and chopped chocolate; spread into pie plate.

Freeze 6 hours or until firm. Remove pie from freezer 10 minutes before serving; let stand at room temperature to soften slightly before cutting to serve.

COWBOY COOKIES

Cream of tartar is the common name for potassium hydrogen tartrate, an acid salt. It helps stabilize and gives more volume to beaten eggs whites and produces a creamier texture in desserts.

2   sticks margarine, softened
1   cup vegetable oil
1   cup packed brown sugar
1   cup sugar
1   egg
2   teaspoons vanilla
3½ cups all-purpose flour
1   teaspoon baking soda

1   teaspoon salt
1   teaspoon cream of tartar
1   cup rolled oats
1   cup crispy rice cereal
1   (12 ounce) package semi-sweet
    chocolate chips
¾   cup pecans (optional)

Preheat oven to 375 degrees. Cream margarine and oil. Beat in brown sugar and sugar. Add egg and vanilla. Combine flour, baking soda, salt, and cream of tartar. Gradually add to creamed mixture. Stir in oats, rice cereal, chocolate chips, and pecans. Drop dough balls by teaspoonfuls onto a greased baking sheet. Bake at 375 degrees for 10-12 minutes. Cool on wire rack.

YIELD: 4 DOZEN COOKIES

If omitting pecans, add ½ cup rice cereal.

CHESS SQUARES

1   package yellow cake mix
½   cup margarine
4   eggs, divided

1   (8 ounce) package cream cheese
1   box powdered sugar
1   teaspoon vanilla

Mix cake mix, margarine, and 2 eggs together, and spread in a 9 x 13-inch pan. Combine cream cheese, powdered sugar, 2 eggs and vanilla. Spread on top of other mixture. Bake at 350 degrees for 40-50 minutes.

LINZER TART COOKIES

2	sticks margarine		3½	cups flour, divided
¾	cup sugar		1	teaspoon baking powder
2	eggs			Jam or preserves
1	teaspoon vanilla			Powdered sugar

Cream margarine and sugar until light and fluffy. Mix 3 cups flour with baking powder; set aside. Add eggs and vanilla to creamed margarine, continue to blend, add flour mixture. Chill dough for 30 minutes in refrigerator. Preheat oven to 350 degrees. Roll out dough, using remaining flour if dough is sticky. Use cookie cutters in shape of your choice to make cookies. Use a thimble or lipstick cover to make a small hole in the center of half the cookies. Place on cookie sheets. Bake for 10 minutes or until cookies

are done, but not browned. Cool completely. Spread jam or preserves on the cookies without the holes, dip cookie with cut out into powdered sugar and place on top of cookies with jam.

HONEY-ROASTED PEANUT CRISPS

1	stick margarine, softened		½	teaspoon baking powder
½	cup vegetable shortening		¼	teaspoon salt
1	cup firmly packed brown sugar		1	cup honey roasted peanuts
1	large egg		1	cup white chocolate chips
1	teaspoon vanilla			Sugar for garnish
2	cups all-purpose flour			

Beat margarine and shortening with an electric mixer at medium speed until creamy. Gradually beat in brown sugar. Add egg and vanilla and beat well. Combine flour, baking powder, and salt. Gradually beat into creamed mixture. Stir in peanuts and white chocolate chips.

Shape dough into 1¼-inch balls. Place 2-inches apart on an ungreased baking sheet. Press each ball down with the palm of your hand. Sprinkle with sugar. Bake at 375 degrees for 8 minutes or until edges are golden browned. Cool slightly on sheet. Cool completely on wire rack.

YIELD: 28 COOKIES

Desserts

DATE BALLS O'FIRE

Perfect for Tu B' Shevat!

¼   **cup creamy peanut butter**
¼   **cup honey**
½   **cup chopped dates**
¼   **cup wheat germ**

½   **cup rolled oats**
¼   **cup semi-sweet chocolate chips**
½   **cup coconut**

Heat peanut butter and honey in a saucepan until honey melts. Add dates, wheat germ, oats, chocolate chips, and coconut. Cook and stir 1 minute. Cool. Roll mixture into balls. Refrigerate for several hours before serving.

YIELD: 25-30 BALLS

TENNESSEE TOFFEE

Some historians believe that the airtight tin was invented in the 1830s for the purpose of storing toffee and other innovative hard candies that were coming into vogue.

3   **cups pecans, toasted and chopped, divided**
1   **cup sugar**
3   **sticks butter or margarine**

2   **tablespoons light corn syrup**
1-1½ **cups semi-sweet chocolate chips**

Spread 2 cups pecans on a lightly greased baking sheet. Combine sugar, butter or margarine, and corn syrup in a heavy saucepan. Bring to boil, stirring constantly. Cook, but do not stir, about 15 minutes until mixture is lightly browned. Pour mixture over pecans. Sprinkle with chocolate chips. Let stand 20 seconds or until slightly melted. Spread chocolate evenly with a knife. Sprinkle with 1 cup pecans. Refrigerate for 2-3 hours. Break into bite size pieces. Store in an airtight container.

YIELD: 20 SERVINGS

TOASTED SPICE PECANS

*Toasting brings out the richness of the nuts' flavor.
When possible, toast all nuts for recipes that do not incorporate
them into the cooking process, such as, salads and garnishes.*

2	cups pecan halves	½	cup sugar
4	tablespoons butter or margarine	1	teaspoon cinnamon
1	egg white	⅛	teaspoon ground nutmeg

Preheat oven to 325 degrees. Spread pecans in a shallow pan. Toast at 325 degrees for 10 minutes. Add butter or margarine to pan. Return to oven to melt butter or margarine. Stir to coat pecans. Beat egg white in a bowl until foamy. Beat in sugar, cinnamon, and nutmeg. Pour over pecans. Bake at 325 degrees for 30 minutes, stirring every 10 minutes. Cool. Store in an airtight container.

YIELD: 2 CUPS

NASHVILLE NUTS

*Use this recipe as a base from which to experiment. Play around with
different types of nuts and spices. Some possibilities: peanuts and cashews, cinnamon and
vanilla or chili powder for a sweet and spicy version. A batch scooped into a
pretty tin makes a great gift or use them as a garnish on cakes, yogurt or trifle.*

1	stick butter or margarine	1	teaspoon salt
2	egg whites	1	pound pecans halves
1	cup sugar		

Preheat oven to 325 degrees. Melt butter or margarine in a 13 x 9 x 2-inch baking dish or jelly roll pan in the oven. Beat egg whites until stiff. Gradually beat in sugar and salt until thickened. Stir in nuts. Spread nuts into dish over butter or margarine. Bake at 325 degrees for 15 minutes. Stir mixture. Bake an additional 15 minutes. Turn off oven and let sit for 15 minutes. Spread nuts out on wax paper to cool. Break apart.

YIELD: 20 SERVINGS

Desserts

228

Epilogue

"My husband would show up at the dormitory at the school every week with freshly baked breads and pastries, and that's when he officially became known in the community as Uncle Meyer," says Eva Rosenberg, recalling the relationship the Rosenbergs had with the students at the Margolin Hebrew Academy. Meyer and Eva owned Meyer's Bakery, the first kosher bakery in Memphis, and the source of breads for students at the school for years. Today, Uncle Meyer and Eva welcome students into their home after services on the Sabbath for *Kiddush*, followed by a piece of Eva's signature angel food cake.

Uncle Meyer and Eva are not just more names in a book; none of the individuals recalled here today are merely fantastic cooks with a plethora of recipes to share. The names you just read, the lives you just heard about, this glimpse into our Memphis community cannot convey the full story behind *Simply Southern with a Dash of Kosher Soul.* So, let us allow a final voice to be heard, with a story that begins years ago with a box.

Before these recipes filled this cookbook, they were passed along in index boxes that the ladies of the school sold. Every Sunday, volunteers went into school and cooked and sold food to the public to raise money for the school. They also organized a cooking school that took place at different homes, teaching Jewish women and non-Jewish women the recipes. The recipe author became the teacher for the day, and everyone brought their cards, followed along and took notes. It was a fun activity and helped support the school through additional card box sales.

Pearl Katz, of blessed memory, conceived of the idea of turning the card box into a cookbook and selling it for the school. The ladies of the community put the book together and when they sold out that printing, they would do a reprint with new cover designs and make changes and additions to the existing book. There were 3 incarnations of this original cookbook. The last rendition of the book was put together by Pearl and her committee of women who had worked on this cookbook for 25 years. In developing *Simply Southern with a Dash of Kosher Soul*, the committee's first step was to reach back into prior versions of the cookbook and include many of the recipes that are considered our community's treasured heirloom recipes. We have worked diligently to ensure that Pearl's voice is heard loud and clear and her vision has never been articulated clearer than in the book you have just finished reading. And now that you know about our culinary heritage, y'all come down for a visit and tell them Pearl sent you.

C

Index

233

Index

Index

Index

239

Index